B·U·S·I·N·E·S·S
Venture

Oxford University Press, Walton Street, Oxford OX2 6DP

Oxford   New York   Toronto
Delhi   Bombay   Calcutta   Madras   Karachi
Petaling Jaya   Singapore   Hong Kong   Tokyo
Nairobi   Dar es Salaam   Cape Town
Melbourne   Auckland

and associated companies in
Berlin   Ibadan

Oxford is a trade mark of *Oxford University Press*

© Oxford University Press 1989

ISBN 0 19 832745 5

For Anne

Printed in Great Britain by
Ebenezer Baylis & Son Ltd. Worcester

PAUL COATES

B·U·S·I·N·E·S·S
Venture

Oxford University Press

Acknowledgements

This book is based on a curriculum development project conducted at Paddington College in London. The course design was produced by the project team as a whole, and individual members of the team then contributed detailed material for me to use in writing the book.

As the co-ordinator of the project, I should like to pay the fullest possible tribute to the work of the members of the project team. This book owes a great deal to their skill, experience and commitment as teachers. It was a pleasure to work with such colleagues.

Team members Anat Arkin, April Cameron, Ian Charles, Sarah Downs, Alicia Fahim, Brian Gallagher, David Ingram, Juliana Johnson, Chrissie Kerr, Christine Lentzos, Barbara Payne, Paul Phillips, Laurian Prout, David Rice, Paulina Sagoe, Yvonne Webb, Pat Wooding.

Specific contributions

Introductory Activity (Creating an Exhibition)	Anat Arkin, Chrissie Kerr and Paul Phillips
Charity Fund-Raising	Juliana Johnson and Laurian Prout
Student Advice & Information Centre	Christine Lentzos
Student Publication	Anat Arkin
Bookkeeping & Calculations	Paul Phillips
Keyboarding & Typing	Paulina Sagoe
IT & Computers	David Rice
Business Organisation information	Yvonne Webb
Law and Trade Union information	Christine Lentzos

Additional contributions, for which I am very grateful, were made by Barrie Clark, Keith Friend, Noneen Jacques, and Owen Mbilizi.

My thanks are due to my colleague, Jean Shirley, who originally suggested this publication to OUP, and to Rob Scriven of OUP for his very helpful encouragement and, not least, his patience. I am grateful to the many students whose uninhibited comments on this material proved so useful in developing it. Equally, I want to acknowledge the innovative and supportive ethos of Paddington College and the Inner London Education Authority, which plays such an important part in enabling teachers to develop improved approaches to their work.

I owe a particular debt of gratitude to my partner Anne Shivas for advice, encouragement and support in ways too numerous to mention, and also to many friends and colleagues at Paddington College whose constant interest and encouragement ensured that I completed this book and lost a year of my leisure time.

For help with the word processing of the text I am indebted to my fellow Amstrad enthusiast, Ian Charles, and his generosity in undertaking essentially tedious work. Lastly, and least, I should also acknowledge the continual contributions of two enthusiastic feline word processors, always too eager to lend a helping paw, Bow and Jo-Boots.

Paul Coates

Teacher's introduction

Aims of the book

This book has two primary aims. The first is to make business studies interesting by enabling students to learn through carrying out simple business activities for themselves. Business information and procedures are presented in the form of instructions for each activity. The instructions include detailed guidance on how the students can operate as a rudimentary administrative organisation within the classroom. This allows different students to work on different tasks, which is useful for students who have different interests or different levels of attainment and need individual learning programmes.

The second aim is that students should develop a critical understanding of the nature of business and its economic, social and political significance; a business studies course which does no more than teach a set of office procedures can scarcely be regarded as educative. It is emphasised that the way in which business is organised, whether by market forces in the private sector or by community planning in the public sector, is a reflection of fundamentally different motivations and values, and leads to very different types of society, government, employment and life opportunities.

The two aims reinforce each other. Tackling real business ventures in the classroom raises, in a vivid and direct way, issues of organisation, procedures, financing, motivation and profit-making, and these issues are all addressed in detail.

How to use the book

The book can be used in various ways.

* **A complete business studies course.** The Contents pages can be regarded as a year plan which indicates the sequence of skills and knowledge to be learnt and the progression from introductory activities with games and simulations to real business ventures. The activities can be treated as course assignments held on particular dates or weeks or in weekly timetabled periods, and subject teachers can prepare students for particular aspects of the activity. For example, in preparation for the Leisure Centre simulation, the Numeracy teacher would help students learn the procedures for producing the Leisure Centre's invoices and calculating the percentage discounts.
* **Specific project work** within a business studies course.
* **The basis of Mini-Co and Mini-Enterprise projects.** The book is useful because it provides very detailed practical guidance on setting up and operating a business organisation. It also provides suggestions for projects which do not require students to spend most of their time in producing goods or services.
* **For real or hypothetical ventures.** Although it is not recommended, the students could, for example, work through all the stages of organising an imaginary day trip, if for some reason it was not possible for them to go on a real trip.

General notes

1 The teacher needs to be thoroughly familiar with the material, especially the educational objectives of each activity, and to decide for themselves exactly how to use it in the classroom. All the activities can be adapted and extended in numerous ways.
2 The Standard of Living Game and the Reference section need to be particularly stressed since they are the basis for understanding the nature of business, and they are referred to repeatedly throughout the book.
3 The assessment profiles provided at the end of each main chapter can also be used at the start of each chapter to reveal the student's learning needs and to emphasise the learning objectives of the activity.
4 The use of "they" instead of "he or she" is deliberate, as discussed on p. 98.

Introduction

This book enables students to learn about business by carrying out real business activities for themselves. No prior knowledge of business or office procedures is needed. At first, the activities are very simple, but they gradually become more complex as business skills and knowledge are introduced.

Introductory activity

Activity 1

This activity provides a basic understanding of the economy and the nature of business and administration. It indicates what sorts of jobs are available and whether they will suit the student. The exhibition acts as a focus to the activity.

Business and administrative activities

Activities 2 and 3

Students set up an administrative organisation, and then practise administrative procedures by running an imaginary leisure centre.

Activities 4 to 8

The administrative organisation is then used to operate real administrative and business ventures. These activities do not need to be followed in the order given. If students have not acquired the skills and knowledge for a particular activity, they can carry out the activity using simpler skills and knowledge, or they can refer to relevant skills and knowledge sections in other activities.

Students work in different departments of the organisation for different lengths of time according to their particular course interests.

Contents

Introductory activity: Creating an exhibition	10
The Standard of Living Game	11
Surveying the local economy	17
Jobs in business and administration	21
Personal qualities	25
The exhibition	28

Exploratory activities

Instructions for Activities	Skills and Knowledge				
	BUSINESS COMMUNICATIONS	BUSINESS CALCULATIONS	BUSINESS PROCEDURES	KEYBOARDING & I.T.	
2 Setting up the organisation What different departments do; roles, equipment, materials, files and forms, etc. Some simple administrative tasks to test organisation's effectiveness.	Layout and design p. 40 Memo p. 42	Petty cash p. 46	Organisational structure p. 34 Reception p. 36 Stock-control p. 45 Filing p. 43	How to operate a keyboard p. 38	33
3 Leisure centre Running an imaginary leisure centre [bookings, equipment hire, enquiries, complaints, special functions etc].	Telephone p. 53 Letters p. 61	Percentages p. 59	Invoices p. 58 Mail p. 52	Typing, layout, and display p. 54 Touch-typing p. 55	49
4 Events Organising school/college events [open days, parents evenings, social/theatrical evenings, discos ... etc, including students union and staff functions].	Meetings Agenda and minutes p. 66	Costing and Pricing p. 69 Accounts — Analysed cash book Bank account Receipts and payments account p. 73	Types of business organisations p. 70 Meetings p. 66 Banking p. 70	I.T. in business p. 74 Word-processing p. 75	63
5 Student travel agency Educational and pleasure visits and trips. Administration on behalf of school/college and commercial ventures selling to students, teachers, parents, local groups, etc.	Questionnaires p. 80 Reports p. 81 Reference Books p. 82 Publicity materials p. 84	Graphs and charts p. 83	Market research p. 80	Databases p. 85	77
6 Charity fund-raising A variety of ventures from simple Bring-and-Buy Sale to helping in running of High Street charity shop.				Spreadsheets p. 90	87

Reference

This section contains background information which is in addition to the skills and knowledge sections of each activity.

	BUSINESS COMMUNICATIONS	BUSINESS CALCULATIONS	BUSINESS PROCEDURES	KEYBOARDING & I.T.	
7 Student advice and information centre Finding out and presenting information on such topics as employment rights, health and safety at work, trade unions, consumer issues. (A way of learning more about business and administration.)			Employment Rights p. 94 Trade unions p. 95 Health and safety at work p. 96 Consumer rights p. 100 Organisational structure p.102	Viewdata systems p. 103	91
8 Student publication Publishing, 'printing' and distributing a student newspaper/magazine/handbook, and bulletins for societies or departments. Selling advertising space.			Reprographics p. 110	Desktop publishing p. 111	105

Reference section	112
Outline of the economy	112
Central and local government	116
Organisations in the British economy	119
Structure of organisations	120
Trade unions	121
Employment law	122
Consumer law	124
Notes for the teacher	
How to organise the leisure centre simulation	125

Creating an exhibition

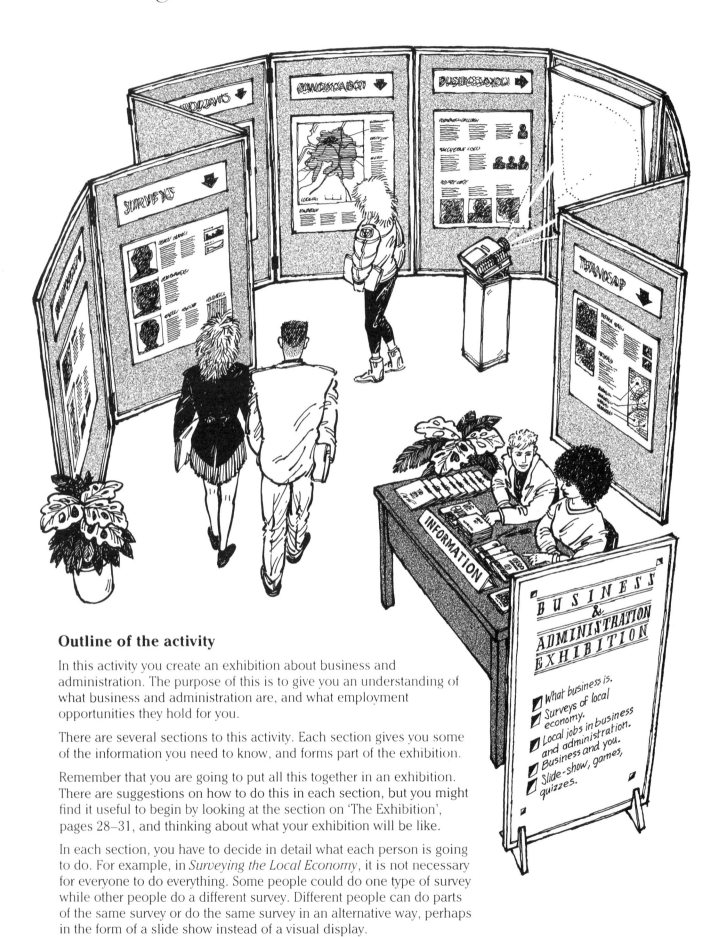

Outline of the activity

In this activity you create an exhibition about business and administration. The purpose of this is to give you an understanding of what business and administration are, and what employment opportunities they hold for you.

There are several sections to this activity. Each section gives you some of the information you need to know, and forms part of the exhibition.

Remember that you are going to put all this together in an exhibition. There are suggestions on how to do this in each section, but you might find it useful to begin by looking at the section on 'The Exhibition', pages 28–31, and thinking about what your exhibition will be like.

In each section, you have to decide in detail what each person is going to do. For example, in *Surveying the Local Economy*, it is not necessary for everyone to do everything. Some people could do one type of survey while other people do a different survey. Different people can do parts of the same survey or do the same survey in an alternative way, perhaps in the form of a slide show instead of a visual display.

The Standard of Living Game

A game for six players which shows how the economy works.

To play this game you need:

- six players and someone to be the timekeeper and referee,
- a table big enough for everyone to sit round,
- a clock or watch,
- blank cards or pieces of paper about the size of playing-cards, and pencils or pens to write on the cards.

Situation

Six families are shipwrecked on an uninhabited island without any food, equipment or possessions. You are the head of your family. It includes old and young, sick and healthy members. All the families work equally hard.

The island

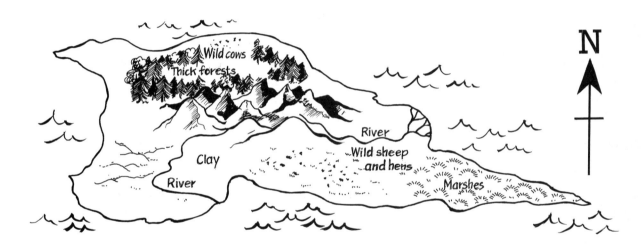

Start of game

Each family looks after itself, trying to produce the food, clothing and equipment it needs. This is difficult. You manage to catch some wild hens for eggs. You make crude cooking-pots from clay. Occasionally, you manage to knit a piece of clothing from sheep's wool.

So, at the start of the game your family's *standard of living* is:

- 1 basket of eggs
- 1 chicken
- 1 piece of knitted clothing } per month
- 1 cooking-pot
- 1 bundle of firewood

The families decide to increase their standard of living by *specialising*. Each family specialises in producing just *one* type of thing. For example, one family concentrates entirely on producing eggs. They become very good at this, producing large amounts of eggs because they do nothing else; they are *specialists*. They then trade some of their eggs with other families to get the other things they want. If they want some firewood, they swap some eggs with the firewood family. This sort of trade is called *barter*.

How to play

The object of the game is to increase your standard of living. The player with the highest standard of living at the end of the game is the winner.

Each round is in two parts. The timekeeper starts and stops each part.

5 minutes *production*

You write on your cards what you have produced in one month. See the detailed instructions for individual players.
IMPORTANT: Each round = one month. You must write out only the correct number of cards for each round.

10 minutes *trading*

You trade some of your month's production, i.e. your cards, with other players. Try to get as good a deal as possible. Remember you are trying to increase your standard of living as much as you can.

The Market place

Where people meet to trade goods

PLAYER 1 *Detailed instructions*	**PLAYER 2** *Detailed instructions*	**PLAYER 3** *Detailed instructions*
You specialise in keeping **HENS** Each round (each month) write out 10 cards ONLY	You specialise in making **TOOLS** Each round (each month) write out 2 cards ONLY	You specialise in making **POTTERY** Each round (each month) write out 4 cards ONLY

Rounds 1 & 2 You produce EGGS

 For each round, mark your cards like this.

Rounds 3 & 4 If people now have enough eggs, you can produce chickens.

 You can play CHICKEN cards instead of EGGS cards.

ALSO

 You can play PILLOW cards instead of EGGS cards.

Rounds 1 & 2 You produce AXES

 For each round, mark your cards like this.

Rounds 3 & 4 If people now have enough simple tools, you can produce more advanced tools.

 You can play HAMMER cards instead of AXE cards.

ALSO

 You can play KNIFE cards instead of AXE cards.

Rounds 1 & 2 You produce COOKING-POTS

 For each round, mark your cards like this.

Rounds 3 & 4 If people now have enough cooking-pots, you can produce crockery.

 You can play CROCKERY cards instead of POT cards.

ALSO

 You can play STORAGE JAR cards instead of POT cards.

PLAYER 4
Detailed instructions

You specialise in gathering
WOOD
Each round (each month)
write out 10 cards ONLY

Rounds 1 & 2 You produce FIREWOOD

1 bundle firewood

For each round, mark your cards like this.

Rounds 3 & 4
If people now have enough firewood, you can produce timber for building huts.

1 pile building timber

You can play BUILDING TIMBER cards instead of FIREWOOD cards.

ALSO

1 set furniture wood

You can play FURNITURE WOOD cards instead of FIREWOOD cards.

PLAYER 5
Detailed instructions

You specialise in
COWS
Each round (each month)
write out 1 card ONLY

Rounds 1 & 2 You produce a COW

1 cow

For each round, mark your cards like this.

Rounds 3 & 4
If people now have enough cows, you can produce leather instead.

1 piece leather

You can play a LEATHER card instead of a COW card.

ALSO

1 churn milk

You can play a MILK card instead of a COW card.

PLAYER 6
Detailed instructions

You specialise in making
WOOLLEN CLOTHES
Each round (each month)
write out 5 cards ONLY

Rounds 1 & 2 You produce SWEATERS

1 sweater

For each round, mark your cards like this.

Rounds 3 & 4
If people now have enough SWEATERS, you can produce woollen TROUSERS.

1 pair trousers

You can play TROUSERS cards instead of SWEATER cards.

ALSO

1 blanket

You can play BLANKET cards instead of SWEATER cards.

Timekeeper		Start time	Finish time
Round 1	Production		
	Trading		
Round 2	Production		
	Trading		
Round 3	Production		
	Trading		
Round 4	Production		
	Trading		

The timekeeper gives each player the correct number of blank cards for each round.

Continuing the game

Rounds 5 & 6

If you continue the game, you will discover more features of the economy. There are some new developments.

> Play as before, following the individual player's instructions below. The timekeeper must ensure that you collect the right amount of blank cards for each round. Use the same scoring system.

1. When you have obtained a complete set of tools, i.e. an *axe* card, a *hammer* card and a *knife* card, your monthly production is *doubled*. Show your cards to the timekeeper to collect twice as many blank cards.
2. There are now some problems in your economy. You have to deal with these by deciding, as a group, to pay some people to provide services instead of producing goods.

Player 1
Instructions
Round 5 A quarter of your production is stolen. The number of cards you can collect from the timekeeper is reduced to 7.
At the next trading session, suggest that someone is paid to provide a police service.
Round 6 If there is now a police service you can collect your usual ten blank cards from the timekeeper.

Player 2
Instructions
Round 5 You have to spend half your time educating your children, so your monthly production is halved. The number of cards you can collect from the timekeeper is reduced to 1.
At the next trading session, suggest that someone is paid to provide an education service.
Round 6 If there is now an education service, you can collect your usual two blank cards from the timekeeper.

Player 3
Instructions
Round 5 Many members of your family are ill. You spend half your time looking after them, so your monthly production is halved. The number of cards you can collect from the timekeeper is reduced to 2.
At the next trading session, suggest that someone is paid to provide a medical service.
Round 6 If there is now a medical service, you can collect your usual four blank cards from the timekeeper.

Player 4
Instructions
Round 5 Half of your production is stolen. The number of cards you can collect from the timekeeper is reduced by half. At the next trading session, say that you will provide a police service. Then you will no longer be able to produce wood, so you will need the other players to pay you the equivalent of 10 wood cards each month.
Round 6 Collect your pay from the other players.

Player 5
Instructions
Round 5 You lose all your possessions in a flood. Return all your cards to the timekeeper; you do not receive any cards for this round. At the next trading session ask the other players for charity (to give you some of their cards).
Round 6 Collect your usual number of cards from the timekeeper.

Player 6
Instructions
Round 5 At the next trading session say that you will provide an education and medical service. Then you will not be able to produce any goods, so you will need the other players to pay you the equivalent of 5 woollen clothes cards each month.
Round 6 Collect your pay from the other players.

Scoring: finding the winner

The winner is the person with the highest standard of living.
Work out a scoring system so you can decide who has the highest standard of living. It cannot just be the person with the most cards, because some cards are worth more than others. A *cow* card must be worth more than an *eggs* card. As a group decide how much each card is worth.
Write down the value of each card.

EGGS		AXE		POT		FIREWOOD		COW		SWEATER	
CHICKEN		HAMMER		CROCKERY		TIMBER		LEATHER		TROUSERS	
PILLOW		KNIFE		JAR		F. WOOD		MILK		BLANKET	

What this game shows

This game is a miniature economy. To understand what the game shows, you need to think about what has happened in the game and to analyse the results. Answer each question and then compare your answer with the *Outline of the Economy* on pages 112–118. Each numbered section in the *Outline of the Economy* provides the answer to the question of the same number on this page.

1. When people landed on the island, they had no food, no shelter, no fuel — nothing. How did they manage to get these things? Similarly, how have all the goods and wealth that we see about us today been created?

2. Using your scoring system, work out what each family's standard of living was before the start of the game (monthly production of each family as described on p. 11).
   Now calculate how much each family produced during Round 1 (total monthly production ÷ six players). What caused the monthly production to increase?

3. What have you invented by devising your scoring system?

   How did you decide how much each card was worth? Was it:
   ☐ How useful or desirable you thought each thing was?
   ☐ How much work has gone into making it, ie how many could be made in a month?
   Is this a fair system for deciding how much people get paid for their work? How are levels of pay decided in our own society? Are they decided by market forces, that is, by supply and demand (see p. 113). Are they also influenced by people's attitudes about how much pay different jobs deserve?

4. Work out how much each family produced, on average, in Round 5 *or* 6 (total monthly production ÷ six players). What has made this different from the amount that each family could produce in Round 1?
   Hint Find out who had the biggest production and ask them how they managed it.

5. What decides which goods (eggs OR chickens OR feathers) are produced?

   What determines the price at which people's produce (eggs, chickens, etc.) is sold?

6 So, why are some rock stars paid more for an hour's work than a nurse is paid for a whole year's work?

6a Is this a good way of deciding what should be produced and how much people are paid? Should everyone be paid the same hourly rate? If not, why not?

7 Write down each player's final score, that is, the total value of cards acquired by the end of the game. Then draw the person so that their score is shown by their height. A high score is a tall person. Half that score would be a person half the height, etc.

For example	
46	72
Player 1	Player 2

Player 1	Player 2	Player 3	Player 4	Player 5	Player 6

This is what happens in a market economy: there are winners and losers, rich and poor. Is this a good idea? Do people have to be in competition with each other? Do you agree with the idea that people should get more if they are born clever, and less if they are born handicapped?

How to present this information in the exhibition

You can use the information you have gained in this game to carry out the surveys of the local economy in the next section. There are also some additional ideas in *The Exhibition*, pages 28–31.

How realistic is this game?

In playing this game, you have created a miniature market economy. You may be interested in some of the things it shows about you and your classmates, and therefore about the society we live in. Look at the following features of your results and ask yourself how realistic they are.

1 How realistic are your results in question 7 above? Is our society really like this? Are the winners that much bigger than the losers? Look at p. 114, *The Income Parade*, to see what the real results are.

2 In your results, what sex were the people with the highest and lowest scores? If there are sex patterns in the results, why should this be? Are there similar patterns in the real world? Do males and females have equal opportunities in your classroom? Which sex does most of the talking and demands most of the teacher's attention? Try considering ethnic minorities in the same way.

3 Look again at *The Income Parade* on p. 114. Where do you, and your parents and grandparents, appear in it? Where will your children appear in it? Why is this? Why is it that doctors and lawyers tend to be the children of doctors and lawyers? Is it just a coincidence, or is it something to do with advantages and unequal opportunities?

Surveying the local economy

In the previous section we looked at the economy as a whole. Now that you have some understanding of what an economy is and how it works, you can examine an actual economy, the economy in your local area.

You do this in three ways:

1 **A map survey** in which you produce a large map of your area. This shows what different areas are used for, the main types of production, and how goods and people are moved about the area.
2 **A street survey** in which you take one street and show the different types of organisations in it and how they fit into the overall economy.
3 **An employment survey** in which you show the main patterns of employment in your area.

You put these three surveys together for the exhibition. Remember that in addition to display boards, you can also present the information in:
- slide shows with a recorded commentary of words and music,
- short talks,
- displays of various items, such as examples of local advertising, publicity materials, packaging and goods.

For further ideas on how to present the exhibition, see pages 28–31.

The map survey

You produce a large detailed map of your area showing the features of the local economy, that is, the way in which land is used and the transport facilities.

Getting your map

It must be large. A black-and-white map may be easier to use because you can shade in certain areas with colour. On a coloured map, use ribbon or tape to outline areas.

Good places to get a map are:
- Your college or school (try the geography department).
- The local council (see below). This is likely to be the most useful map you can get.
- A good bookshop. A road-map or street plan may be best, but there are many other types which may also be useful for information.

You can either use a printed map or you can draw your own based on a printed map.

Illustrate your map with photographs or examples of products, packaging, and advertising.

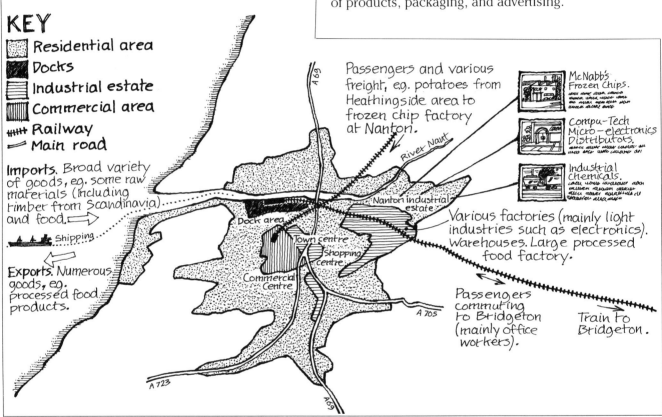

Where to get the information

Your local authority (See Reference section on page 119 if you are not sure what this is.) Local authorities often have *Information* or *Public Relations* departments which provide information about the area covered by the authority. They usually have maps, guides, leaflets, fact sheets, perhaps a *Borough Handbook*. This would provide much of the information you need.

Libraries Your school or college library, and especially the local reference library, will have lots of information. Take these instructions with you and show the librarian what type of information you are looking for. Some of the following books may be helpful:
local tourist guide books, up-to-date geography books, introductory sections of local directories, such as the telephone books *Yellow Pages* and *Thomson Local Directories*, and local trade directories.

Your own knowledge You will already know some of this information simply through living in the area. Think about what you know and what you can work out as a matter of common sense.

Teachers See what information teachers may be able to give you.

Visits You can find out a great deal by going and looking. Take a bus ride round an industrial estate to see what sort of factories there are. Look to see what goods are being carried on trains and trucks.

See also the Reference page Outline of the Economy, page 112.

The street survey

You produce a survey of a local street to show the types of organisations in the local economy.

Choose your street carefully. Try to find one with many different types of organisations: offices, shops, factories, government departments and so forth. When you have decided on your street, walk down the street with a clipboard, recording the sort of details shown here.

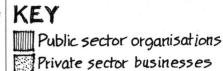

KEY
- Public sector organisations
- Private sector businesses

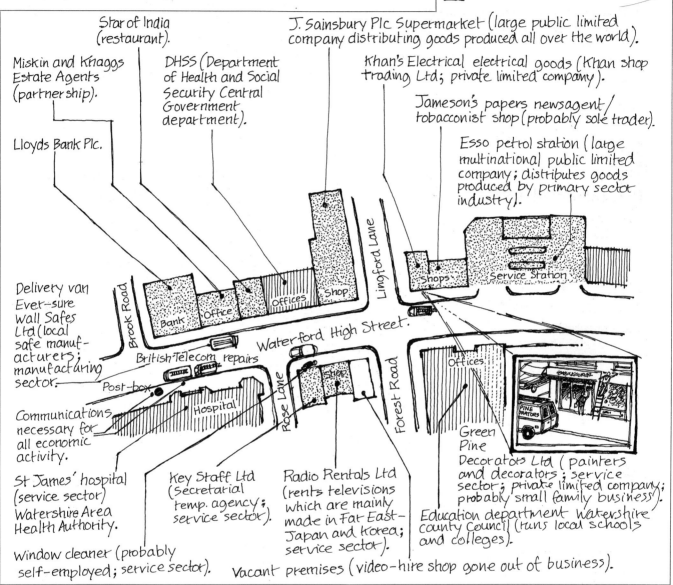

The information you need

1. What each building or piece of land is: office, shop, factory, etc.
2. The name of the organisation.
3. The type of organisation it is (the Reference section on page 119) will help you). Look for information on notices and signs. Find out more information by looking up the organisation's name in the *Yellow Pages* or trade directories.
4. The activity you see: transport, people working, communications, etc.
5. Add notes explaining how the organisations and activities shown in your survey are part of the economy.
6. Illustrate your street survey with photographs or advertisements relating to the organisations shown in your survey.

The employment survey

In this survey you show some of the main types of employment in your area.

Where to get the information

Libraries Ask the librarian for information on local employment patterns and national youth employment. Say that you would like the information in a simple, straightforward form, perhaps in magazine articles or local authority publications. If that is not available you can get the information from standard reference books such as *Regional Trends* (published by HMSO) although you may need help from your teacher. MSC (Manpower Services Commission) regional publications are particularly useful.

Local employers Any large employer will usually have an information department which will be able to give you information leaflets about the organisation. They may also be able to arrange a tour of their premises. If you are able to visit or tour an employer's premises, see if you can collect leaflets and take photographs.

Careers teachers Careers teachers and careers service staff are an excellent source of information about local employment.

Job advertisements Job advertisements in local newspapers and job centres will give you some idea of the main types of employment. For example, you can count up the number of vacancies advertised in different types of employment.

How to present the information

To show facts and figures use different types of charts and graphs. See page 83 for information on how to draw graphs and charts.

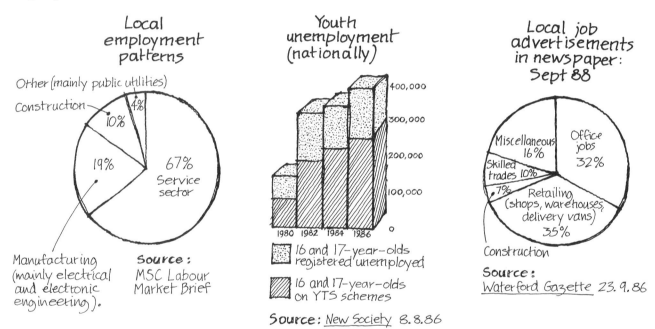

Information about employers can be presented in writing illustrated with photographs, leaflets, advertisements and examples of products and packaging.

Jobs in business and administration

In this activity you find out about the types of jobs in business and administration.

They can be in any organisation that needs an office to keep things organised: local councils, companies, large stores, travel agents, hospitals, factories, and small businesses.

How to find out about these jobs

1 Look at pages 22–3 which describe the basic types of jobs.

2 Look at the job advertisements in the local newspapers and the job centre. Notice:
   • the job title: receptionist, filing clerk, etc.
   • what the person has to do in the job: dealing with enquiries from the public, filing medical records, etc.
   • what age and qualifications are expected.

3 Visit your local careers service or talk to your careers teacher to get more information. See if it is possible to visit or speak to the personnel department of a large local organisation to find out what types of office jobs are available.

4 Find someone who has an office job, and interview them. This could be a friend, relative, day-release student in your college, or someone in your school or college office. Your teacher may be able to help. If possible try to visit the person at work and get them to show you what they do. These are the sorts of questions you could ask them:

   What is their job title?

   What do they do in their job? Make sure they list **all** the things they do.

   How long have they been in their job?

   What qualifications and experience did they need to get the job?

   Do they enjoy it?

   What do they like most and least about it?

   Are there any promotion prospects?

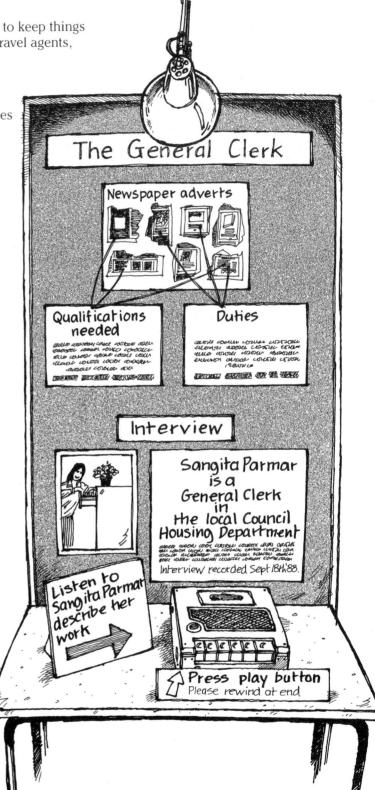

Hints
Cut out newspaper job advertisements.
Collect any relevant leaflets.
Make a tape recording of your interview.
Take photographs of the person at work.
You might find it useful to look at *Types of organisations* and *Organisation structures* in the Reference section of this book.

Types of job

These are the main types of business and administration jobs open to you when you first start work after an introductory business studies course.

After some years of work, and especially if you study for further qualifications, you could apply for more senior jobs. See page 24 for details.

Clerk typist

This job would involve you in two different types of work: straightforward typing, such as letters or forms, and general duties, such as answering the phone and filing. A clerk/typist job would suit someone who did not want just to type all day. There are many different kinds of clerk/typist jobs and some will involve more or less typing or clerical work than others. People who enjoy a variety of tasks each day are well suited to this kind of work. There are usually opportunities for promotion, especially if you stay with the same company.

Trainee/office junior

Many firms expect staff to start at the bottom and work their way up; this is exactly what an office junior, or trainee, will do. It will first involve doing a little of everything, and gradually learning how the office and the business work. Typing, photocopying, filing, answering the phone, sending off the post each day, and simple administrative tasks are the kinds of job undertaken by an office junior. The opportunities for promotion and/or branching out into particular areas are usually good, especially if you are willing to take further part-time studies.

Receptionist

This job is mainly about dealing with people. You would make appointments for clients and deal with enquiries. There could be some other work as well, such as typing or filing. You would need to be trained to operate a telephone switchboard. The most important feature of this work is getting on with people, so it is best suited to someone who is polite, can speak clearly, has a neat appearance and a pleasant manner. Some businesses, for example, hotels, would probably only take on someone with specialist training in receptionist duties.

Office machine operator/VDU operator

Depending on the type of organisation, machines will be used in one way or another to help run the business. For example, a VDU operator works a keyboard connected to a computer; it is very different from an ordinary manual or electric typewriter. This type of work mainly involves feeding information into a computer. A Telex machine is also very common in the modern office, and you might be trained to use one. Someone with typing ability should find it easier to learn to use office machinery.

Typist

You will need some qualifications in typing before you can apply for typing jobs. Specialist qualifications, such as RSA (Royal Society of Arts) certificates, demonstrate that you have achieved an adequate level of speed and accuracy.

Jobs range from working in a typing pool, carrying out general typing duties, to being attached to one person or office, therefore it is very important to select the type of work which interests you. Some people start off as typists and end up as office managers. Your chances of promotion are helped if you are prepared to work hard, and demonstrate your ability.

General clerk

Here you might be working only in one particular area of an organisation. You could be called the office junior. You might have to work with figures. Nearly all firms employ some kind of clerk, and most of the training is done 'on the job'. This work would suit someone who is neat, well-organised, enjoys writing, and perhaps is also good at dealing with people on the telephone. Again, there may be good chances of progressing to other work, such as personal assistant.

Future prospects

The jobs shown on the previous two pages can be interesting and enjoyable, and you may be quite satisfied to remain in such jobs for many years, especially if you like the office you work in and the people you work with.

On the other hand, you may be interested in more senior jobs which present you with additional challenges and pay higher wages. There are two possible routes to such jobs: 'working your way up' in employment, or further full-time study.

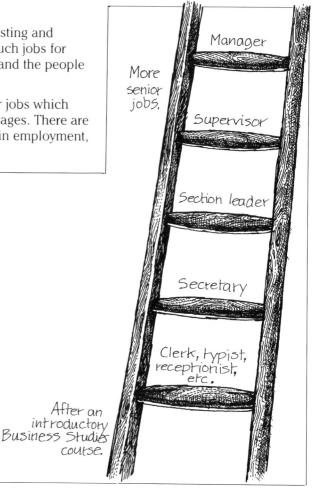

Progress through employment

What you need to progress:

Personal qualities You need to be keen, hard-working and determined. You need to show that you have ability, and that you can work well with other people.

Further part-time study Day release or evenings at College, or company training courses will help you considerably. It is essential for some jobs.

The type of senior job you reach depends on the area of work in which you gain experience and promotion, eg in Accounts, or Sales, or Personnel Departments, and on the type of organisation you work in. For example, senior jobs in local government are very different from senior jobs in an estate agents.

The size of the organisation may affect your prospects.

Large organisations	Small organisations
• Many jobs, so promotion prospects are better. • Want to train and promote their own staff. • Often have a definite career structure (although it can be rigid). • Specialist personnel departments to oversee training and promotion of staff. • Greater chances of day-release and company training schemes.	• Fewer jobs, so promotion prospects often depend on someone leaving. • No personnel department, so less supervision and support in career development. • You may have to move between firms to gain experience. • On the other hand, you may get broad experience of all aspects of the work because there are only a few employees, eg in an estate agent's office, and this may provide rapid career progress if you show ability.

Progress through further full-time study

Introductory Business Studies Course
- Advanced General Business Studies courses, eg BTEC National, sometimes with specialist options
- Secretarial courses, eg leading to RSA qualifications in Typing and Office Practice
- Specialist vocational courses, eg retailing, travel and tourism, computer usage

Personal qualities

What sort of person are you?

Different jobs in business and administration require different qualities (see the previous section on pages 22–3). In some you need to be very well organised and to work on your own keeping accurate records. In others you may spend most of your time in speaking to people, and you need to be friendly, patient and able to explain things clearly.

Self-assessment quiz

This is a quiz which helps you to think about what sort of person you are, so that you can match your personal qualities to those required by different jobs. Don't take the quiz too seriously; it is just meant to set you thinking about what sort of job would suit you best.

Look at each of the following eight situations. Note the answer of your choice for each situation.

Situation 1

Your company is making a special offer to all customers who have spent more than £500 with your company in the last six months. Your office is asked to notify these customers of the special offer. Do you offer to:

a) *Check through the files to find out which customers should be notified?*

b) *Type a standard letter to be sent to each customer?*

c) *Go to the post office to buy the stamps for the letters?*

d) *Notify each customer by telephone?*

Situation 2

You and another person in your office apply for promotion and you do not get it. Do you:

a) *Decide your best prospects are to look for another job?*

b) *Feel miserable but try not to let it show?*

c) *Feel miserable and talk to the others in the office about it?*

d) *Ask your boss to tell you why?*

Situation 3

You are busy with your typing when you notice a visitor at the reception-desk waiting for the receptionist. Do you:

a) *Go and find the receptionist?*

b) *Tell your supervisor that there is someone waiting?*

c) *Ask the visitor if you can help them?*

d) *Decide that your job is to get on with your typing, and that the receptionist will return in a moment?*

Situation 4

A customer telephones with an enquiry and wants to speak to your workmate, who appears to be taking a rather long lunch break. Do you:

a) *Ask the customer if you can help them with their enquiry?*

b) *Say you cannot find your workmate at the moment?*

c) *Tell the customer your workmate is late back from lunch and ask them to call again later?*

d) *Say your workmate is out of the office and offer to take a message?*

Situation 5

Your supervisor is out of the office for the afternoon and has left you a number of fairly urgent tasks to work on. However you are interrupted in your work by numerous phone calls, and you realise you will not be able to finish all the jobs by the end of the day. Do you:

a) *Ask your colleagues to answer the phone calls to leave you free to get on with the other jobs?*

b) *Ask your colleagues if they would do some of the other jobs?*

c) *Decide for yourself which are the most urgent jobs and make sure you get those done?*

d) *Decide that you are not expected to be superhuman, and simply deal with the telephone calls while fitting in the other jobs as best you can?*

Situation 6

One of your jobs is to keep a record of money spent on postage stamps used by several people in the office. You discover that there is something slightly wrong with the figures: the number of stamps that are left does not quite match the amount of money spent. Do you:

a) *Quietly tell your supervisor that you suspect someone is stealing stamps?*

b) *Check with the other people how many stamps they have actually used?*

c) *Check all your figures again and again until you find out exactly what has happened?*

d) *Ask your supervisor whether it matters since it is only a very small difference in the figures?*

Situation 7

You are asked to make photocopies of an announcement about a fire-alarm practice and to distribute them to everyone in your office. But while you are using the photocopier it runs out of paper. You do not know how to load more paper into the machine. Do you:

a) *Do some other work and leave the photocopying until later when someone has put some more paper in the machine?*

b) *Ask someone to show you how to load the paper?*

c) *Read the instruction manual to find out how to load the paper?*

d) *Decide it will be easier to tell everyone verbally about the fire-alarm practice?*

Situation 8

Your supervisor asks you to go to the stock-room and count up the stationery supplies. You find the room in a mess with many boxes of stationery in the wrong places and half-empty. You realise it will be a long job. Do you:

a) *Decide that it is only fair that the person who left the stock-room in a mess should be asked to tidy it up, so that you can make an accurate count of the stationery supplies?*

b) *Spend some time tidying up the stock-room before counting the stationery supplies?*

c) *Instead of counting every single item, and in order not to be a long time carrying out the job you have been asked to do, make sensible estimates of the amounts of stationery?*

d) *Ask you supervisor for some help to tidy the stock-room?*

How to analyse your answers

To find out what your answers tell you about yourself, simply use this profile grid.

PERSONAL QUALITIES PROFILE								
	SITUATIONS							
	1	2	3	4	5	6	7	8
Level 4	b	d	c	a	c	d	b	d
Level 3	a	b	d	b	a	c	c	b
Level 2	d	c	a	d	b	b	d	c
Level 1	c	a	b	c	d	a	a	a

High profile

You are suited to *all* types of office jobs. You are good at dealing with people, and you are also good at record-keeping and paperwork. You are able to work on your own responsibly, but you also know when to seek help and guidance from others.

Medium profile

You have the personal qualities needed for *some* types of office jobs.

Level 3 answers suggest you avoid dealing with people and prefer to work on your own. You would be good at jobs involving record-keeping and paperwork. Perhaps you need to develop your skills and confidence in dealing with people.

Level 2 answers suggest you are good at dealing with people, whether they are workmates or customers. However, you tend to avoid record-keeping and paperwork. Perhaps you should try to take a greater interest in these areas.

Low profile

Level 1 answers suggest you are tending to avoid office work altogether. This could mean you are not really suited to this type of employment, or it could be that you have not fully realised what is involved in business and administration jobs.

Study your profile and see if you think it is accurate. If there are some answers which do not seem to fit the pattern of the profile, have another look at those situations and decide what your answers tell you about yourself. You may find it helpful to do this with a friend and analyse each other's profiles.

Remember **not to take this quiz too seriously. If may not be at all accurate. It is only intended to help you think about what your personal strengths are, what qualities you should try to develop in your course, and what type of business and administrative job might suit you.**

The exhibition

You are going to create an exhibition about business and administration, based on this activity. The exhibition will describe what business and administration are, how they are part of the economy, and what job opportunities they offer.

Who to invite You need to decide who you are going to invite to the exhibition, because this will help you to decide how to design the exhibition. The main visitors are likely to be other students and staff in your school or college. The exhibition would be very useful for students who might be interested in careers in business and administration. However, you could also invite parents and friends.

What to put in the exhibition You should include all sections of this activity:
- The Standard of Living Game
- The surveys of the local economy
- Jobs in business and administration
- Personal qualities quiz

How to put these things into the exhibition

You can have:

☐ **Visual displays** These are likely to be the main part of your exhibition. Each section of this activity contains suggestions and ideas for visual displays. Remember that these can include tape recordings as well as pictures and writing. (See page 17 for an example.)

☐ **Photographic displays/slide shows/ videos** You will probably have some photographs in your visual displays, but you can also have a special photographic section of the exhibition. This would be a series of photographs with just enough writing (headings, titles and captions — notes under each photographs) to explain the photographs. If you want to be more ambitious, you could produce a slide show or even make a video.

☐ **Activities** You can make the Standard of Living Game and the Personal Qualities Quiz part of the exhibition. It will help visitors to understand what business and administration are, and what personal qualities are needed.
For the game, set out tables, instructions and blank cards for visitors to play the game. Make sure you can explain to them what the game shows about the economy.
You can make Personal Qualities part of the exhibition either by simply providing copies of the quiz, or by offering interviews based on the quiz followed by a discussion of job possibilities based on displays of job advertisements.

☐ **Events** You can include special events, such as a visiting speaker or the showing of a film or video. The visiting speaker could be a local employer talking about the job opportunities in their organisation, or perhaps someone from the Careers Service. The film or video would need to be related to the theme of the exhibition: the nature of business, commerce, the economy and employment in administration. It would need to be a film or video which visitors to your exhibition would find interesting and enjoyable.

Finding out about exhibitions

You can get more ideas for your exhibition by visiting other exhibitions and seeing how they have been created.

You will be able to find exhibitions in local libraries, museums, art galleries, town halls, and in local organisations of all sorts. To find out about exhibitions in your area, look in the local paper, enquire at libraries, and look at notice-boards in libraries and other public buildings.

When you visit an exhibition make a note of:
- How it has been publicised
- What sort of room or hall it uses
- How it has been arranged
- What sort of signs and notices it has
- How the items in the exhibition have been displayed
- The opening times and staffing

PUBLICITY How has the exhibition been publicised? How did you find out about it? What posters, leaflets, newspaper advertisements or articles are there? How are they designed and worded? (Collect samples if possible.)

PREMISES What sort of room or hall is the exhibition in? Furniture, decorations, natural or artificial lighting?

LAYOUT How has the entrance to the exhibition been arranged? Is there a reception or information desk? How has the room been set out? (Draw a simple diagram) Any background music or sounds?

NOTICES AND SIGNS How have they been made? What materials have they used? How are they fixed in position?

CONTENTS What is there in the exhibition? (Visual displays, photographs, film, video, sound, models, diagrams, activities for the visitors?)

DISPLAYS How and where have the contents of the exhibition been displayed? Look at the display boards and see how they have been made. See how items have been fixed to the wall or shelves or stood upright. What materials have been used: glue, tape, pins, cardboard, wood, fabric? What sort of lighting is used?

MANAGEMENT What are the dates and opening hours of the exhibition? Are there any staff in attendance? Do they answer questions and explain the exhibits?

How to set out the exhibition

Premises

Your exhibition can be set up in a hall, a classroom, or even along a corridor. It is important that the premises are as empty and bare as possible so as to focus people's attention on your exhibits. Try to remove, or shift to one side, any furniture, notices, or decorations which are not connected with your exhibition.

Times

It can be an exhibition which is open all day for several days, or just for one afternoon, or perhaps every lunch-time for a week. You may be able to leave your exhibits in place from one day to the next, or you may need to put them away at the end of each session.

Equipment

Work out what equipment you will need. This could be tables, chairs, display-boards, projectors, screens, videos, lighting, cassette-recorders, extension leads, and stationery.

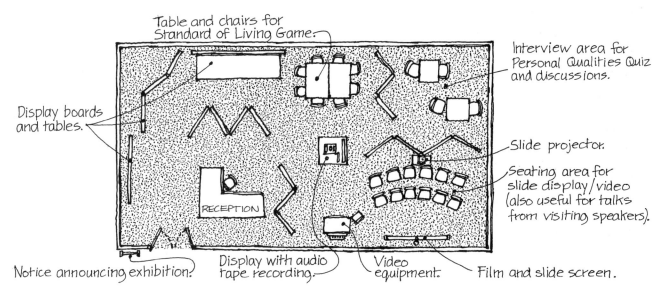

The exhibition set up in a hall

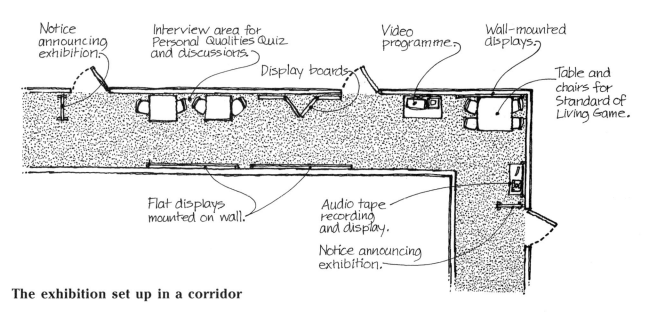

The exhibition set up in a corridor

Displays

It is very important that your exhibition looks smart, professional, and business-like, even if you only have limited resources. The important thing is to see what you can do with the resources you have.

Display areas

You must have *large blank areas* in which to mount your displays, otherwise your displays will not stand out. There are various ways of achieving this.

- **Walls** If you have plain, pale, blank walls like an art gallery you can mount your displays directly on the wall. You may be able to make your walls, or sections of them, like this by covering them with large sheets of plain paper or fabric.
- **Display-boards** See if your school or college has any display-boards, that is, any type of movable notice-boards on which you can pin notices and visual displays. They could be boards which stand up on their own, or which need to be attached to the wall, or placed on tables.
- **Make your own display-boards** You can create display-boards out of any large flat materials. If you cannot find suitable materials in your school or college, you may be able to borrow them, or you might be able to buy them: large sheets of polystyrene or soft notice-board material are not expensive. Here are some suggestions.

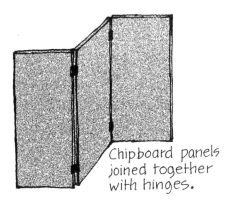
Chipboard panels joined together with hinges.

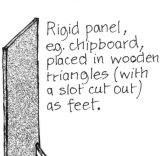
Rigid panel, e.g. chipboard, placed in wooden triangles (with a slot cut out) as feet.

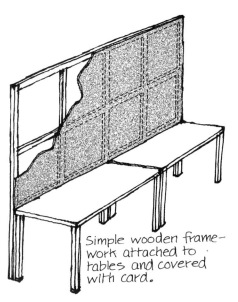
Simple wooden framework attached to tables and covered with card.

Mounting displays

To make your displays, use paper for the writing, typing, pictures, chart and diagrams. Then glue the paper to thick, heavy sheets of card.

Lighting

A final professional touch is to light your displays with spot-lamps. It will dramatically improve their appearance. If your school or college does not have spot-lamps, see if you can borrow some from home. Use as many spot-lamps as you can and reduce the room lighting.

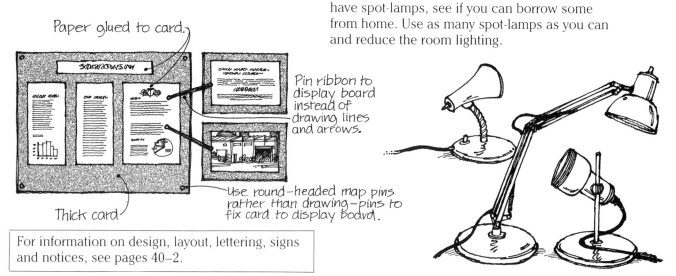

Paper glued to card.
Pin ribbon to display board instead of drawing lines and arrows.
Thick card
Use round-headed map pins rather than drawing-pins to fix card to display board.

For information on design, layout, lettering, signs and notices, see pages 40–2.

Publicity

You can publicise your exhibition in various ways:

- **Notices, posters and leaflets** The leaflets can be smaller versions of the posters.
- **Circular letters** to group tutors and parents.
- **Announcements** Ask group tutors to tell students about the exhibition in tutorial sessions, or you could arrange to visit different classes yourselves to make brief promotional announcements.

Make sure your publicity is lively and enthusiastic. Remember to include all the necessary information, such as dates, times, and location.

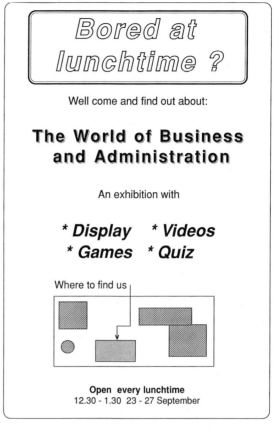

Managing the exhibition

1. Decide what your exhibition will be like.

2. Obtain all the necessary approvals and permission. Book the premises, equipment and any storage facilities you will need.

3. Decide who is going to do what, and when each piece of work needs to be ready. A *flow chart* like this will help you plan.

	Monday	Tuesday	Wednesday
Group 1	Send off film for processing	Collect film	Mount photographs onto display-boards
Group 2	Make display-boards and erect them in exhibition room		Mount writing and diagrams onto boards
Group 3	Make publicity materials	Obtain spot-lamps	Arrange lighting of exhibits

4. Follow the detailed instructions for each section of the exhibition (pages 28–31).

5. Set up the exhibition, and draw up a rota of people to staff the exhibition. They will need to be able to answer questions and talk to visitors about the exhibition, as well as looking after the exhibits and equipment.

6. Dismantle the exhibition and return the equipment.

Assessment profile

This profile helps you assess what you have learnt in this Activity. You should aim to have achieved at least Level 2 in every section, and Level 3 in most sections. Work with a colleague to fill in the profile, making sure you can convince your colleague that you have achieved each level. Tick each level that you have achieved.

	Level 1	Level 2	Level 3	Level 4
Understanding the economy Production	Can explain how goods and services are produced in a simple economy.	Can explain how specialisation, money and capital operate.	Can describe the main features of an advanced economy such as Britain's.	Have identified features of the British economy in the local area.
Understanding the economy Different economic systems	Can explain what is meant by an economy.	Can explain meaning of 'market economy', 'planned economy' and 'mixed economy'.	Can describe the main features of these different types of economic systems.	Can offer opinions with reasons on merits of different types of economic system.
Understanding the economy Types of organisations	Can give some examples of different types of business organisations.	Can explain the difference between private sector and public sector.	Can list the main types of organisation in the private and public sectors.	Can explain and discuss the different purposes and motivations of the different types of organisations.
Employment in the local economy	Can give some examples of typical jobs in the local area.	Can identify the main types of employment and the names of major employers in the local area.	Have produced detailed analysis, with charts, of local employment patterns.	Can explain how local employment and unemployment patterns fit into the economy as a whole.
Jobs in business and administration	Can name some types of jobs in business and administration.	Can give name and description of main jobs in business and administration.	Can describe the personal qualities, experience and qualifications needed for certain jobs in business and administration.	Have made detailed study of at least one type of job in business and administration.
Personal qualities	Can explain what sort of personal qualities are relevant to employment.	Can identify some of your personal strengths, weaknesses and interests.	Can match up your main personal qualities to those required by particular jobs in business and administration.	Can give detailed reasons for a definite career intention.
Organising an exhibition A typical business activity	Can explain, in outline, what needs to be organised.	Can give detailed account of what is involved in organising an exhibition.	Can explain the importance of being able to work successfully in groups.	Can explain what makes for success or failure in organising.

Date completed _____   Signed _____

Setting up the organisation

You are going to set up a simple office organisation which is able to run various administrative and business ventures. The organisation will have four different departments. You begin by working in one particular department, and when you have learnt all about that department's work you move to another department. You need to work in all four departments of the organisation to find out about all aspects of administration, but you can choose to spend most of your time in those departments that particularly interest you.

What you need

You do not need any elaborate facilities or equipment. You can manage with little more than an ordinary classroom, some typewriters and somewhere to keep your stationery locked away. But the better your facilities and equipment, the more business-like your organisation will be.

	Minimum requirements	*Ideal facilities*
A room	You are going to turn this into an office. Ideally, you will be able to keep this room permanently set out as an office. But if other classes need to use the room sometimes, you may have to rearrange the room each time you use it and store your equipment in a locked cupboard.	
Furniture	Tables (preferably desks) and chairs.	Room dividers as found in open-plan offices, or display-boards. Notice-boards. Easy chairs and low table for Reception.
Equipment Typewriters	Manual typewriters.	A range of manual, electric, electronic, and word processor machines.
Filing equipment	This could be a set of manilla envelopes in a cardboard box, or ring binders and box files.	Proper filing cabinets with suspension files. Filing trays (IN/OUT trays). Card-indexes.
Reprographics	Spirit (Banda) duplicator or access to one.	Spirit and ink duplicators and photocopier, or access to these.
Storage cupboards	Secure cupboard with cardboard boxes for storing stationery.	Additionally, a locked drawer with a cash-box.
Computers	Access to computers with business software.	One micro (or equivalent), located in each department with Prestel. Word Processing, data base, spreadsheet, graphics, view-data and tutorial software.
Telephone		Telephone located in room or nearby.
Stationery	Paper, card, cardboard, envelopes, etc. of all sizes and colours. Pens, drawing pens if possible, pencils, felt-tips, rulers, stencils, transfer lettering (Letraset). Paper-clips, rubber bands, treasury tags, etc. Scissors, hole-punch, stapler, modelling knife, glue (Pritt Stick).	
Miscellaneous	Token (Monopoly) money.	Calculators, reference books. Real money for petty cash (see page 46–7). Postal scales. Date stamp.

Getting started

1. Decide on a name for your organisation. Do this as a class before you divide into departments. (See page 119 for legal requirements.)
2. Decide who is going to work in each department. You could do this by a lottery, or by deciding which department you are most interested in (see next page).
3. Give all the equipment and stationery to the people who are going to be the Records Department; give the money to the Accounts Department people.
4. Follow the instructions for your Department (pages 36–47).

Your organisation

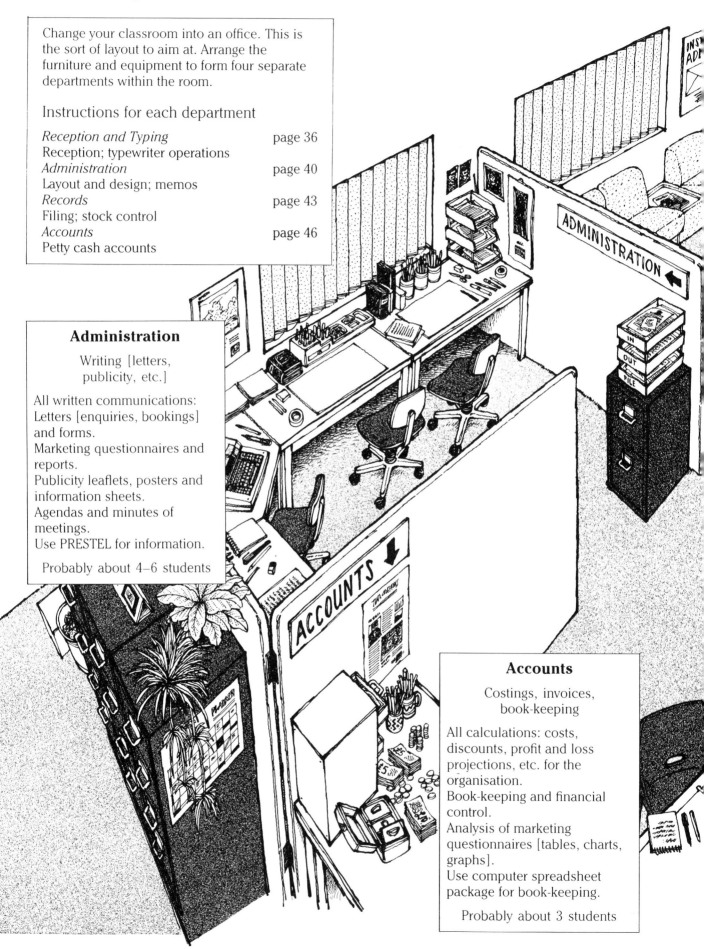

Change your classroom into an office. This is the sort of layout to aim at. Arrange the furniture and equipment to form four separate departments within the room.

Instructions for each department

Reception and Typing	page 36
Reception; typewriter operations	
Administration	page 40
Layout and design; memos	
Records	page 43
Filing; stock control	
Accounts	page 46
Petty cash accounts	

Administration

Writing [letters, publicity, etc.]

All written communications:
Letters [enquiries, bookings] and forms.
Marketing questionnaires and reports.
Publicity leaflets, posters and information sheets.
Agendas and minutes of meetings.
Use PRESTEL for information.

Probably about 4–6 students

Accounts

Costings, invoices, book-keeping

All calculations: costs, discounts, profit and loss projections, etc. for the organisation.
Book-keeping and financial control.
Analysis of marketing questionnaires [tables, charts, graphs].
Use computer spreadsheet package for book-keeping.

Probably about 3 students

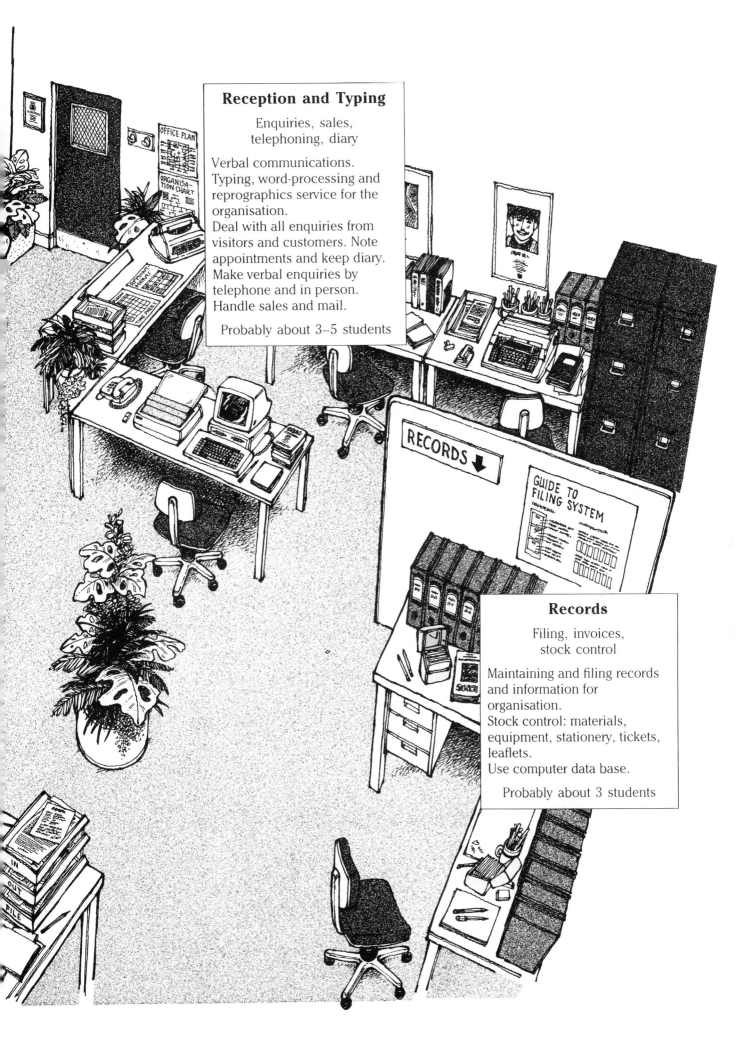

Reception and typing department

The Reception and Typing Department is the organisation's link with the outside world. It deals with visitors, telephone calls, and appointments. It must be able to give a good impression to other people and organisations.

The Department's other important task is to provide the typing and reprographics service which any organisation needs to produce business-like documents.

What to do

1. Arrange your furniture and equipment to create a Reception area and a typing area. See page 34, and below.
2. Decide what notices and signs you want, and send a memo to the Administration Department who will make them for you. (See page 42 for instructions on how to send a memo.)
3. Set up your IN/OUT trays. See page 42.
4. Organise your filing system. See page 43. You will need files for:
   - copies of the memos you send. (Use date order or subject order.)
   - your Reception forms, charts, documents and information.
   You need only keep a few files; give out-of-date documents to the Records Department for filing.
5. Draw up your Reception charts, forms and documents as shown below.
6. Be ready to deal with callers to Reception. Make sure you know how to operate the typewriters and the duplicator or photocopier.

Reception

The reception area is the visitor's first impression of your organisation, so you must design it to be smart, attractive and efficient. Think about how it will appear to the visitor, and what the visitor will need.

Think about what sort of image, the impression of the organisation, you want to project to the visitor. Very formal? Relaxed but efficient? Friendly and informal? There is no *correct* image. Like your personal image, your clothes, hair-style and actions, a business organisation's image depends upon what sort of organisation it is and the type of people it will be dealing with. But remember that you need to get the visitor's confidence and goodwill if they are to do business with you.

Arrange the furniture, the equipment, the desk tops, and your own appearance, to create the image you want.

Operating the reception

If you are to present your organisation to the public, deal with enquiries and make appointments, you need to have up-to-date information about the organisation. These are the documents you will need to produce and use.

Hints

- Outside the door, place a notice which displays the name of the organisation and explains its purpose.
- Make sure that the Reception area is clearly marked (RECEPTION, ENQUIRIES, etc.) so visitors will know where to go.
- Arrange a waiting area for visitors. Provide easy chairs, magazines, an ashtray, and coat-hooks.
- Use the Reception area to promote your organisation by displaying information: organisation charts, office plans, publicity materials and examples of work. Ask Admin. for a large notice explaining what the organisation is and what it does.

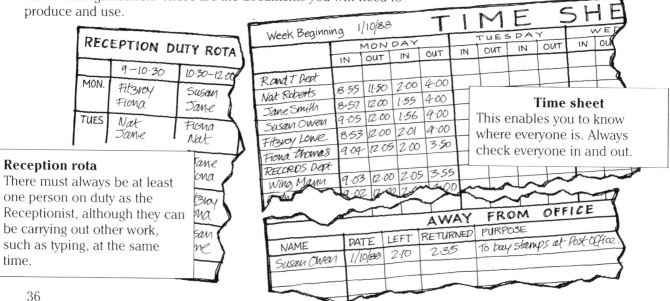

Reception rota
There must always be at least one person on duty as the Receptionist, although they can be carrying out other work, such as typing, at the same time.

Time sheet
This enables you to know where everyone is. Always check everyone in and out.

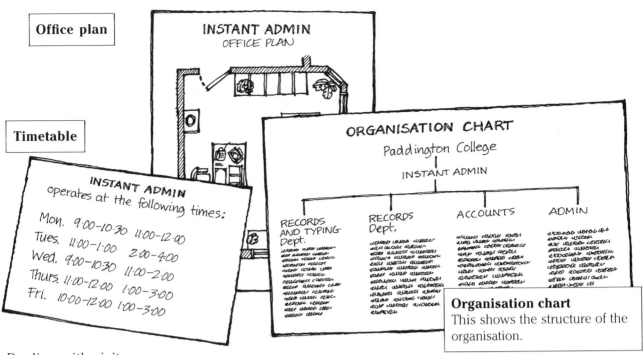

Dealing with visitors

1. Anticipate visitors' requirements. Visitors will be curious about your organisation. So, make sure there is someone available in your department to show them around and explain what each department is doing.
2. When visitors enter, ask them if you can help them. Be friendly and efficient.
3. If they have to wait, offer them a seat. Keep them informed of what is happening, and if they have a long wait offer them a cup of tea or coffee.

These are the documents you will need for dealing with visitors.

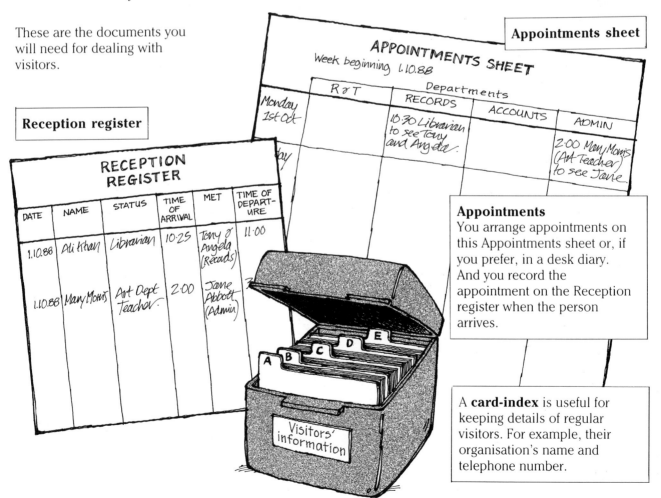

Typing

Anyone involved in business and administration needs to know how to operate a typewriter. You will then be able to produce smart, professional-looking documents when you need to, and you will find it easier to operate computer keyboards.

Typing is easy. It is just a matter of knowing the basic principles and practising them. This page gives you all the information you need to be able to type. Typing layout and touch-typing are covered on pages 54–5.

Learning the controls

To learn how a typewriter works, study this diagram. Then put some paper into the typewriter and try out all the controls. Keep using all the different controls until you are quite sure you know how it all works.

Line space adjuster Adjusts the space between the lines. Set for half, single or double line-spacing.

Put the paper in here, against the roller. The left-hand edge of the paper should be against the paper guide.

Bail bar Keeps the paper pressed flat. Make sure the paper goes underneath it.

Margin stops Press down and slide along to set the left and right margins.

Carriage release Lets you move the carriage from side to side.

Turn this knob to move paper up and down. Hold in and turn for small adjustments.

Carriage return lever Push this right across the typewriter at the end of every line of typing.

Ribbon colour Changes colour of typing if you have a two-coloured ribbon. Sometimes there is a similar lever to make the typing darker or lighter.

Margin release Allows you to type beyond the margin stop.

Shift lock This locks the shift key down, so that you do not have to hold it down. To release it, press the shift key.

Shift key Hold this down while pressing other keys and you will type capital letters and upper case characters, that is, the characters on the upper parts of the number keys.

The basic rule of typing

Leave one space after a comma, and two spaces after a full stop.

Hints

1. Hit the keys sharply, but not too hard.
2. Set left and right margins before you begin typing.
3. Use tab settings to line up columns of typing.

Try this piece of typing [set the margins and tab].

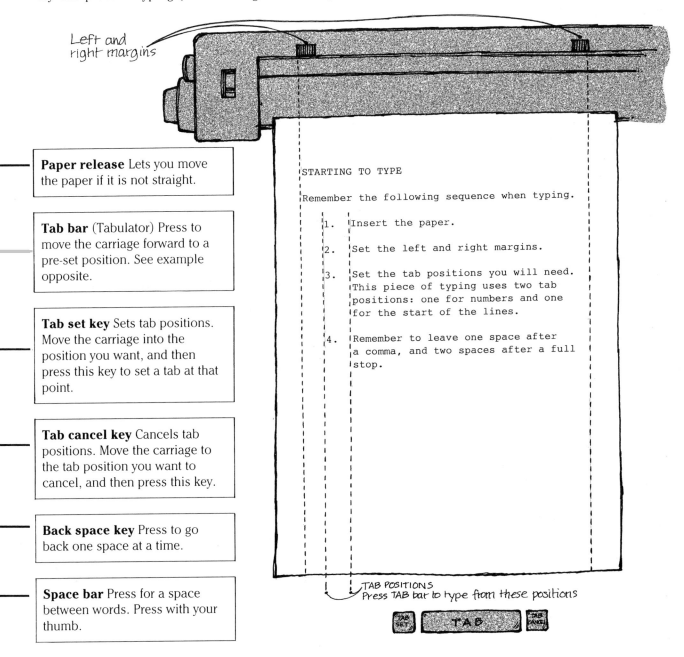

Paper release Lets you move the paper if it is not straight.

Tab bar (Tabulator) Press to move the carriage forward to a pre-set position. See example opposite.

Tab set key Sets tab positions. Move the carriage into the position you want, and then press this key to set a tab at that point.

Tab cancel key Cancels tab positions. Move the carriage to the tab position you want to cancel, and then press this key.

Back space key Press to go back one space at a time.

Space bar Press for a space between words. Press with your thumb.

Electric and electronic typewriters

Operating a typewriter is like driving a car. If you know how to drive, you can drive any car, although some of the controls may be in different places. Manual, electric and electronic typewriters are all basically the same, the controls are simply in different places.

Administration department

The Administration Department specialises in communicating effectively on paper. It needs to be able to produce letters, forms, questionnaires, publicity leaflets and posters which are smart, well-written and professional-looking.

Detailed instructions for producing different types of business documents are given in the following activities. This activity deals with the basic skills of layout and design. These are essential in producing any business document. They are also particularly useful in this activity because one of the Administration Department's first jobs is to create the signs and notices which the organisation needs.

> **What to do**
>
> 1. Arrange your furniture and equipment (see page 34) to create an Administration Department area.
> 2. Set up your IN/OUT trays (see page 42).
> 3. Contact the Records Department and ask them to start collecting and filing examples of layout and design, as described at the end of the Layout and design section below.
> 4. Set up your filing system (see page 43). You will need files for:
>   - copies of the memos you send and receive.
>   - the documents you are working on, perhaps one file for each person or each piece of work.
> 5. Decide what notices and signs you want, and begin to make them. The other departments will send you memos asking you to produce signs and notices for them. Remember that the Reception and Typing Department is able to produce typing for you. Send your requests in a memo (see page 42).

Layout and design

For notices, signs, posters, circulars, letters, memos, forms, information sheets, reports, questionnaires . . . business documents of every kind.

1. **Paper and card** Use good quality, heavy-weight paper or card. Think about the different ways you can use it.

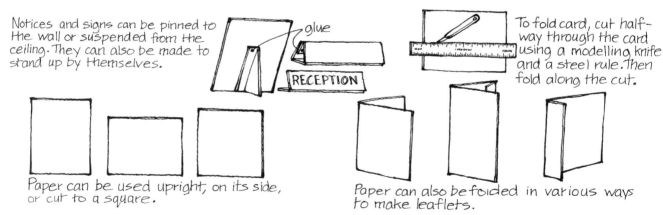

Notices and signs can be pinned to the wall or suspended from the ceiling. They can also be made to stand up by themselves.

To fold card, cut halfway through the card using a modelling knife and a steel rule. Then fold along the cut.

Paper can be used upright, on its side, or cut to a square.

Paper can also be folded in various ways to make leaflets.

2. **Layout** Decide where to put headings, titles and writing, and how to divide up the space with lines, boxes, margins and backgrounds.

3 Lettering If possible use transfer lettering (Letraset, etc.) and a proper drawing pen (Rotring, etc.) for drawing lines and boxes.

When using transfer lettering, draw a pencil line on your paper and  match it up with the line printed under each letter.

If you cannot use transfer lettering, use a good stencil.

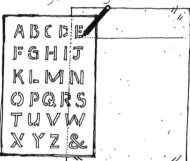

If you have to draw letters, rule two faint pencil lines and make your letters fill the space between them. Then rub out the pencil lines.

Remember that there are different styles of lettering.

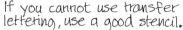

Example of a notice to go on a door.

Use different sizes of lettering and combine it with lines, boxes, margins and backgrounds. Draw faint pencil lines to help you design the layout accurately. Afterwards rub out the pencil lines.

- Coloured card pasted on to thick white card.
- Transfer lettering.
- Margins drawn with a ruler and drawing pen.
- Typing pasted on to coloured card.

Illustrations must look professional. Use transfers, (Letraset, etc.), or trace silhouettes on to coloured card, or use books of copyright-free illustrations intended for photocopying.

To make a logo

A logo (pronounced low-go) is an organisation's symbol which is used on all documents and advertising. It helps to give the organisation an identity, just as you would identify a familiar face.

You can make a logo very easily. Simply arrange the name, or initials, of your organisation in an attractive way and try combining that with a simple pattern. Then run off photocopies of your finished design.

Photocopier paste-up technique

Using this technique you build up the document you want by pasting together different items onto one sheet of paper.

1 Collect the lettering, typing, illustrations, backgrounds, etc. that you want to use.

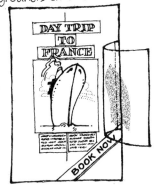

2 Then arrange them on the piece of paper, using faint pencil lines to guide you. You can also add transparent overlays made by rubbing transfer lettering patterns or backgrounds onto O.H.P. sheets.

3 Paste them all together, and make any final alterations with ink and Tipp-Ex. Rub out the pencil lines.

4 Now simply photocopy your pasted-up document. All signs of the paste-up will disappear and you will be left with a perfectly arranged, professional-looking document.

Finding out more

The best way to learn more about layout and design is to study lots of examples of the layout and design of documents. Look at the way the paper has been used: where space has been left, where the paper has been folded, where it has been divided up by lines or boxes, what the background is like, what different sizes and styles of lettering there are, what sort of illustrations there are and how they have been combined with the wording.

The Records Department can obtain examples for you. Ask them to collect as many leaflets, notices, newspaper advertisements, signs, posters, business letters and circulars as possible. They can do this by sending a memo to everyone in the organisation asking them to bring whatever examples of these they can find at home or elsewhere. The Records Department can then file these and look after them. You will have to decide how they should be filed. Here are some suggestions:

Colour leaflets, black-and-white leaflets, single-page leaflets, two-page leaflets, circular letters, letters to individual people, good examples of lines/boxes/margins/bands, interesting/unusual layouts, different lettering styles, etc.

The memo

A memo is a written message to someone in your organisation. It is usually set out in a standard way.

Memos are useful because they are often quicker and more reliable than finding someone and speaking to them in person. They are also a written record. For this reason it is useful to file the memos you receive, and to file the carbon copy of each memo you send. Important memos are usually typed and signed, but routine memos are handwritten.

IN/OUT trays

These are like a two-way letter-box which gives you a link to the other departments. Other departments put documents for you in your IN tray and you put documents in the OUT tray which you are going to take to other departments' IN trays. Documents which you are going to file should be put in the FILE tray.

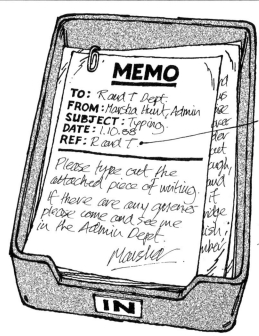

reference number indicates which file the copy of the memo should be filed in.

Records department

To operate effectively, an organisation must be able to keep track of what is happening. This is the job of the Records Department. It has to be able to provide precise detailed information for the rest of the organisation. Although each department will keep a few files, the main centre for records and information is the Records Department.

One of the most important jobs of this Department is therefore to look after the *stock*, the organisation's equipment and supplies. The stock can be worth a considerable amount of money, so it is most important to know exactly what there is, where it is, and to make sure none of it is lost.

What to do

1. Almost immediately, people from other departments will begin to ask you for equipment and stationery. Until you have got your stock control system set up, be sure you make a note of who is given what and ask them to sign the note.
2. Arrange your furniture and equipment (see page 34) to create a Records Department area of the room.
3. Set up your IN/OUT trays (see page 42).
4. Decide what notices and signs you want, and send a memo to the Administration Department who will make them for you. (See page 42 for instructions on how to send a memo.)
5. Organise your stock control system, and your filing system. (See below.) If you want anything to be typed (labels, notices, stock control cards, etc.), or if you want multiple copies of any of these, send a memo to the Reception and Typing Department asking them to do this for you.

Filing: how to keep records

1. Decide what sorts of documents you want to file, and what equipment to use for which files.

Folders. Cheap and simple system, but easily disorganised and soon wears out.

Ring binders. Keep documents securely in order, but very slow to use.

Card-index. For small amounts of information which can be written on a card.

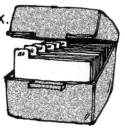

Box files. Not easy to find individual documents. Only useful for storing documents which are only wanted occasionally.

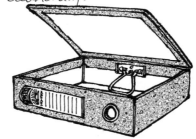

Visible strip-index. For very small amounts of information which can be written on a strip of paper, eg. telephone numbers.

The Records Department should keep these files

Memo file for copies of all the memos you send to other departments and the memos you receive.

Departmental records for each department. The other departments will only keep a few current files and will give their past files to you for storage.

Information files Now, and especially in future activities, your organisation will require information on such things as travel, charities, consumer rights, and examples of graphic design, advertisements and student magazines.

Correspondence files for copies of all the letters sent and received by the organisation.

Stock control files You may prefer to keep your stock control cards all together in a file, rather than individually attached to each stock bin.

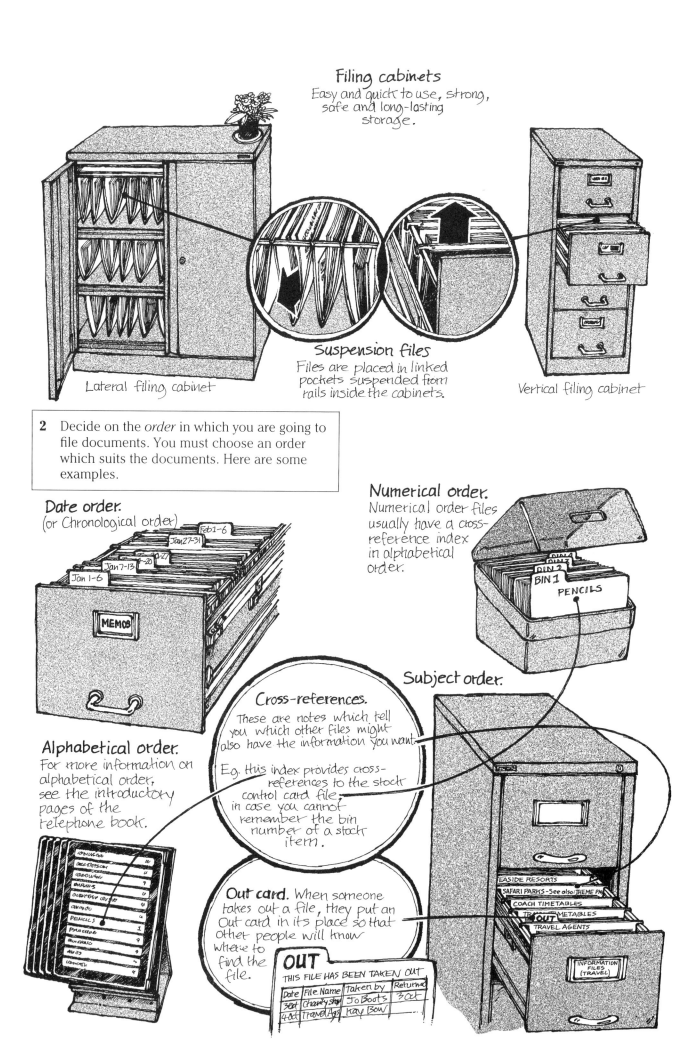

Stock control

1. Make a list, an *inventory*, of all the stock, the equipment, stationery and supplies, so you know exactly what stock the organisation has.
2. Organise your stock cupboard. Find a place for each item of stock. This could be a compartment, box, jar, bin, basket, or other container, but it is always called a *bin* whatever sort of container it is. Label and number each bin. Attach a stock control card to each bin.
3. Make out your stock control cards.

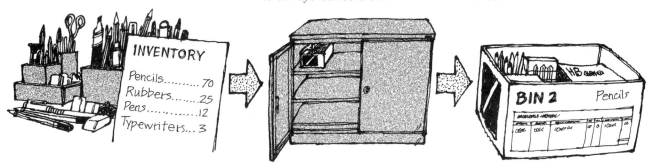

A **stock control card** is a record of that item of stock. To understand how it works, imagine keeping a record of the money you have in your purse or wallet. Read from left to right for each day.

Date	Money put IN to purse	Money taken OUT of purse	WHAT'S LEFT in purse
1 Jan	£10 (from bank)	£6 (bought book)	£4
2 Jan		£1 (lunch) £2 (pen)	£1
3 Jan	£20 (pay)	£5 (record)	£16

A stock control card works in the same way except that the names are slightly different.

Date	IN	OUT	WHAT'S LEFT
Date	RECEIVED	ISSUED (i.e. given out).	BALANCE (i.e. what's left in stock).

STOCK CONTROL CARD

Stock: Pencils
Bin no: 1
Catalogue no: 23A
Supplier: Sarah Jones (Course Tutor)
Delivery: 2 weeks
STOCK LEVELS
Max: 50
Min: 20

Date	RECEIVED Quantity	From	ISSUED Quantity	To	BALANCE
1 Oct.	30	Sarah Jones			
3 Oct.			3	Rot Dept.	27
5 Oct			2	Accounts	25
			5	Records Dept.	20

- Any number you may need to quote when reordering.
- Decide what would be the maximum amount you would want.
- Minimum stock level is the lowest level you let your stock fall to before you reorder. Remember that your minimum stock must last until the next delivery. So calculate:

Minimum = Typical weekly issue × delivery time
= 10 pencils per week × 2 weeks
= 20 pencils

4. Decide which items of stock are to be issued once, eg paper, and which items need to be issued and returned each day or each lesson, eg stapler or hole punch.
5. Periodically, perhaps at the beginning and end of each day or each week, count up the items in each bin and check that this amount agrees with the number on the stock control card. This is called *stock-taking*. You must do this regularly to make sure your records are correct and that stock is not being lost.

Finding out more

You can find out more about filing, classifications, and stock control systems by visiting relevant work places. For instance, you could ask the Librarian at your school or college to show you what systems the library uses. Someone with a Saturday job at a supermarket might be able to arrange for your Records Department to visit the stock area at the supermarket. Your teacher might be able to arrange a visit to a local warehouse. You can find out more about filing equipment by looking at office equipment shops and catalogues.

Accounts department

The Accounts Department plays a crucial role in the organisation: it controls the money. It must know exactly how much money the organisation has, where it has come from, where it is, and what it is being spent on. It must be able to prove that the money is being handled properly so that no one can accuse anyone of stealing, losing or mis-spending money.

What to do

1. Arrange your furniture and equipment to create an Accounts Department area of the room.
2. Set up your IN/OUT trays.

3. Decide what notices and signs you want, and send a memo to the Administration Department who will make them for you.
4. Set up your filing system. You will need files for:
   - copies of the memos you send and receive (use subject order or date order)
   - the petty cash vouchers (use date order)
   - your petty cash accounts (use date order).
5. Draw up forms for petty cash vouchers and a petty cash book. If you want to have the forms typed and multiple copies made, send a memo to the Reception and Typing Department asking them to do this.
6. Before you start keeping the accounts with real money, it is best to practise keeping the accounts with token money. One person should write out the vouchers and 'spend' the money, and another person should keep the accounts.

Petty cash book

Any organisation needs to keep some money in the form of cash. This is the way to look after cash.

1. Put the money in a locked cash-box and keep the cash-box locked away in a safe place, perhaps in a locked drawer during the day, and in the school or college safe at night. You record (*enter*) the amount of money you have in the cash-box in your petty cash account.

   The cash that you start with is called the *float*.

2. When your organisation uses some of the money to buy something, the person who goes to the shop should fill out a *petty cash voucher*, and attach the receipt from the shop.

The *petty cash voucher* is a very important document. It proves what you did with the money, ie gave it to Debbie Jackson, and the receipt proves that she spent the money properly.

You should file these away very carefully in date order.

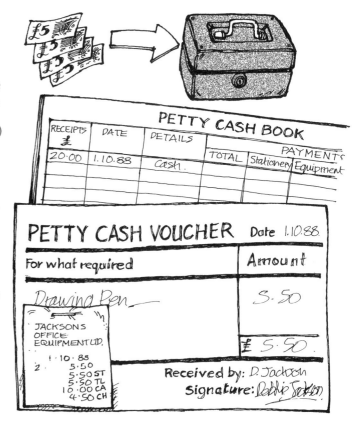

3 Then you record the spending of the money by entering it in your accounts.

PETTY CASH BOOK

RECEIPTS £	DATE	DETAILS	PAYMENTS £					
			TOTAL	Stationery	Equipment	Post	Travel	Misc.
20.00	1.10.88	Cash.						
	3.10.88	D. Jackson.	5.50	5.50				
	4.10.88	A. Khan.	0.45				0.45	
	4.10.88	E. Rowlands.	2.99		2.99			
	5.10.88	J. Lewis	1.28				1.28	

Notice that you record the amount twice: once in the TOTAL column and once in the analysis column.

Analysis columns. These enable you to analyse what you have spent the money on.

4 At the end of each week, or each day or month as appropriate, add up all the columns.

PETTY CASH BOOK

RECEIPTS £	DATE	DETAILS	PAYMENTS £					
			TOTAL	Stationery	Equipment	Post	Travel	Misc.
20.00	1.10.88	Cash						
	3.10.88	D. Jackson	5.50	5.50				
	4.10.88	A. Khan.	0.45				0.45	
	4.10.88	E. Rowlands.	2.99		2.99			
	5.10.88	J. Lewis	1.28				1.28	
			10.22	5.50	2.99		1.73	

5 Now *balance* the payments and receipts. This means subtracting the total payments from the receipts to find out how much money you have left. This is called the *balance*. Then bring the balance down to the next month, and continue as before. Whenever you receive more money, remember to add it into your RECEIPTS column.

It is important to check that the totals of the analysis columns equal the sum of the TOTAL column. You do this by cross-casting (adding sideways across the page).

Important You must check that you have actually got this amount in the cash-box.

c/d means: *carried down* into the receipt column for the next month.

b/d means: *brought down*. The balance from the previous month becomes the receipts this month.

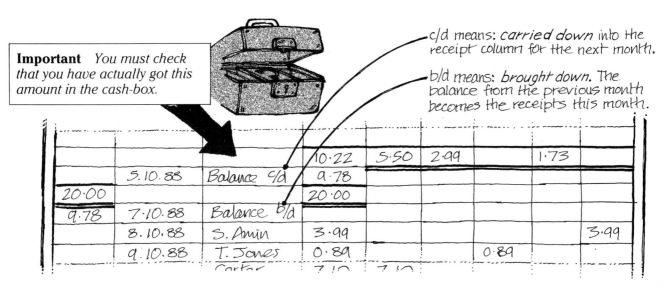

			10.22	5.50	2.99		1.73	
	5.10.88	Balance c/d	9.78					
20.00			20.00					
9.78	7.10.88	Balance b/d						
	8.10.88	S. Amin	3.99					3.99
	9.10.88	T. Jones	0.89			0.89		
		Carter	7.10	7.10				

47

Assessment profile

This profile helps you assess what you have learnt in this activity. You should aim to have achieved at least Level 2 in every section, and Level 3 in most sections. Work with a colleague to fill in the profile, making sure you can convince your colleague that you have achieved each level. Tick each level that you have achieved.

	Level 1	Level 2	Level 3	Level 4
Organisational Structure	Can explain some jobs each Department does.	Can explain what each Department does.	Can explain how each Department's work connects with other Departments.	Can explain reasons for each Department's share of work.
Reception Dept Reception procedures	Can explain how Reception area should be arranged.	Can describe the forms, charts and documents used in Reception.	Can explain how to deal with visitors at Reception.	Have some experience of dealing appropriately with visitors and documents in Reception.
Reception Dept Typing	Can insert paper in typewriter and use basic keys.	Can operate all the controls on a typewriter.	Have typed using *margin* and *tab* controls.	Have produced a short piece of typing smartly set out without mistakes.
Administration Dept Layout and design	Can explain why layout and design are important in business documents.	Can explain what produces an attractive layout and design.	Have produced a smart draft design of leaflet or notice.	Have produced a smart finished leaflet or notice using paste-up technique.
Administration Dept Memos	Can explain what a memo is.	Can explain all the features of a memo.	Can set out memos without using notes or textbook.	Have produced several memos to a business standard.
Records Dept Filing	Can explain what filing is and why it is needed.	Can describe the main types of filing equipment.	Have some experience of keeping different types of files.	Can confidently use all stock control files including cross-references.
Records Dept Stock control	Can explain what *stock control* means.	Can explain basic features of stock control cards.	Can confidently use all sections of stock control card.	Can describe and explain all stock-keeping procedures.
Accounts Dept Petty cash	Can explain what a petty cash system is in outline.	Can explain how the system operates.	Can demonstrate how to fill in the petty cash vouchers and petty cash book.	Have correctly completed and balanced petty cash book several times.

Date completed _____   Signed _____

Leisure centre

Before you begin to use your organisation for real administrative jobs, it is useful to practise administration and learn a few more business procedures. You do this by using your organisation to run an imaginary leisure centre. So, for this activity only, your organisation is the Leisure Centre office.

How your organisation will operate

The Reception and Typing Department receives requests for membership and bookings and sends them to Records. After Records has processed them, they are sent to Accounts, who work out the bills to be sent to the members. Administration writes the necessary letters, which are typed by Reception and Typing.

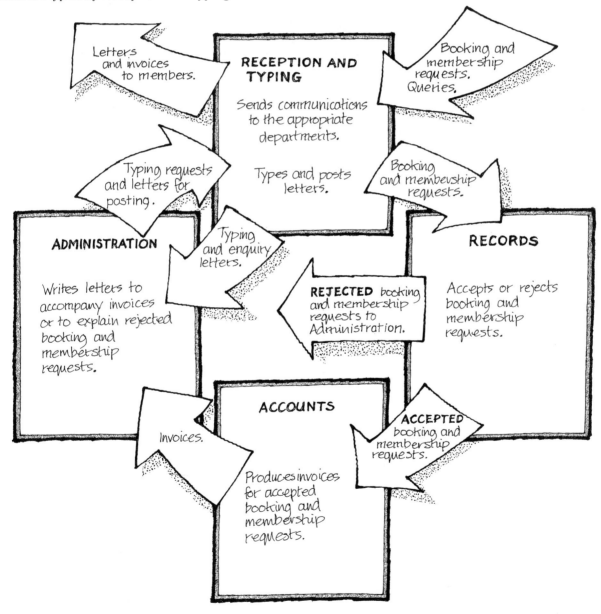

Study the Woodlands Leisure Centre leaflet which is shown on the next page. Then follow the instructions for each Department (pages 52 to 61).

WLC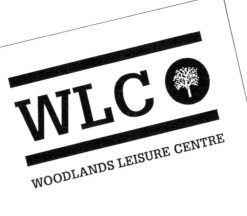
WOODLANDS LEISURE CENTRE

A Leisure Centre providing facilities for local clubs and individuals.

WOODLANDS LEISURE CENTRE

FACILITIES

PLAN OF CENTRE

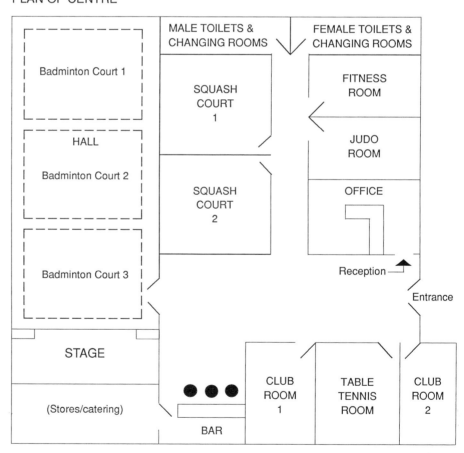

The Leisure Centre has three Badminton Courts, two Squash Courts, and a Table Tennis Room. There is also a Judo Room and a Fitness Room. The Judo Room is available to local clubs for judo classes. The Fitness Room enables members to improve their fitness. It is equipped with exercise bicycles, rowing machines, and weights. Up to four members can use the Room at the same time (ie four bookings per session).

In addition, there are two Club Rooms equipped with tables and chairs. They are available to local societies and clubs for society activities, such as meetings and film shows.

The Hall may be booked for sports, such as five-a-side football, or functions, such as theatrical productions and discos. The stage is fully equipped with professional lighting and sound equipment.

The Bar is open to members and their guests.

BOOKINGS

CHARGES (per 45 minute session)

Badminton Court	£3
Squash Court	£3.25
Fitness Room	£1
Judo Room	£7
Table Tennis Room	£2.50
Club Room	£5
Hall	£15

All bookings should be made RECEPTION, preferably on a Request Form. Members will be in bookings, and invoices should be two days.

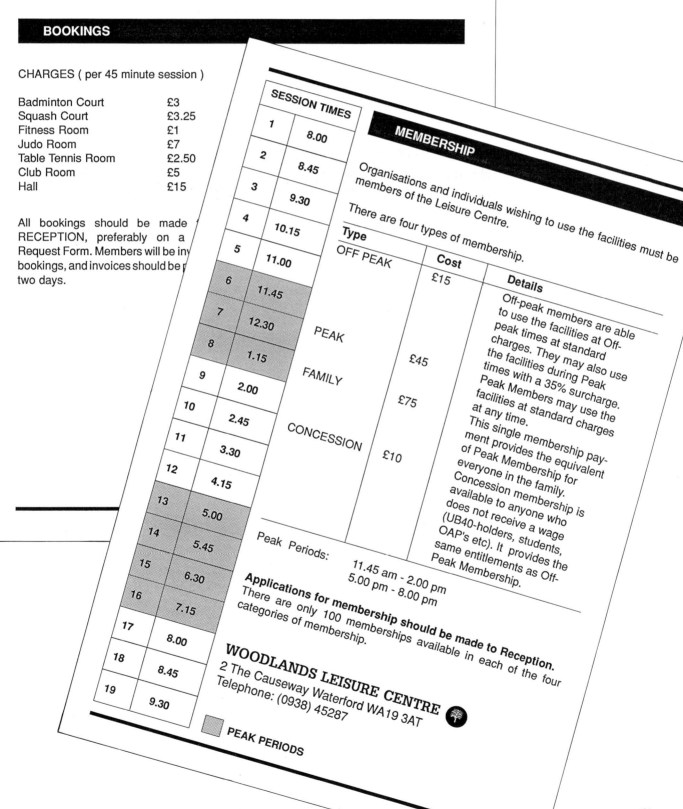

SESSION TIMES	
1	8.00
2	8.45
3	9.30
4	10.15
5	11.00
6	11.45
7	12.30
8	1.15
9	2.00
10	2.45
11	3.30
12	4.15
13	5.00
14	5.45
15	6.30
16	7.15
17	8.00
18	8.45
19	9.30

▓ PEAK PERIODS

MEMBERSHIP

Organisations and individuals wishing to use the facilities must be members of the Leisure Centre.

There are four types of membership.

Type	Cost	Details
OFF PEAK	£15	Off-peak members are able to use the facilities at Off-peak times at standard charges. They may also use the facilities during Peak times with a 35% surcharge.
PEAK		Peak Members may use the facilities at standard charges at any time.
FAMILY	£45	This single membership payment provides the equivalent of Peak Membership for everyone in the family.
CONCESSION	£75	Concession membership is available to anyone who does not receive a wage (UB40-holders, students, OAP's etc). It provides the same entitlements as Off-Peak Membership.
	£10	

Peak Periods: 11.45 am - 2.00 pm
5.00 pm - 8.00 pm

Applications for membership should be made to Reception. There are only 100 memberships available in each of the four categories of membership.

WOODLANDS LEISURE CENTRE
2 The Causeway Waterford WA19 3AT
Telephone: (0938) 45287

Reception and typing department

All communications (letters, telephone calls and visitors) to and from the Leisure Centre pass through Reception. You will receive letters, and you will receive recorded telephone calls, as though recorded on a telephone answering machine. You may also receive a few live telephone calls or personal callers.

All booking and membership matters should be sent to Records; queries about invoices, payments, and money should be sent to Accounts; general enquiries and replies to letters should be send to Administration.

What to do

1 **Recorded telephone calls** Make a supply of *telephone message forms* (See page 53). Listen to each recorded telephone call and write the message and details on a Telephone message form. Then send the message to the appropriate department, as described above.

2 **Mail** Deal with the incoming mail (see below), and send each letter to the appropriate department as described above.

3 **Telephone enquiries and personal callers** Direct them to the appropriate department. See opposite, and pages 36–7 for information on how to deal with visitors and telephone callers.

4 **Type letters** and other documents as requested by other Departments. Always make a carbon copy of a letter and type an envelope for posting it in.

Mail procedures

How to deal with incoming and outgoing mail

A large organisation which receives thousands of letters and parcels every day will have a special Mail Room and staff to deal with the mail. In smaller organisations the mail is usually dealt with by Reception.

Incoming mail

1 **Open each letter** except those marked *Private* or *Confidential* which should be sent directly to the person without being opened. Use an electric letter-opening machine if you have one.

2 **Staple any enclosures to the letter.** There is often something enclosed with the letter in the envelope, perhaps a form or cheque.

3 **Stamp today's date on the letter** or write it on if you do not have a stamp. This shows when the letter was received.

4 **Send the letter to the appropriate department.** Use wire trays for sorting the letters and carrying them to each Department.

Outgoing mail

1 **Check each letter.** Check that it is signed, that the address on the letter is the same as the one on the envelope, and that any enclosure referred to in the letter is attached or is in the envelope.

2 **Fold the letter** and seal the envelope. Try to make no more than two folds.

3 **Weigh each letter** to find out what stamps are needed. You will need to consult a Post Office leaflet. If you have lots of letters and parcels, sort them into groups before weighing them.

4 **Put the stamps on.** Many organisations use a *franking machine* instead of stamps, because it is much quicker.

5 **Post the letters**. Sort them into separate groups: First Class, Second Class, etc., if they are to be posted into different post-boxes.

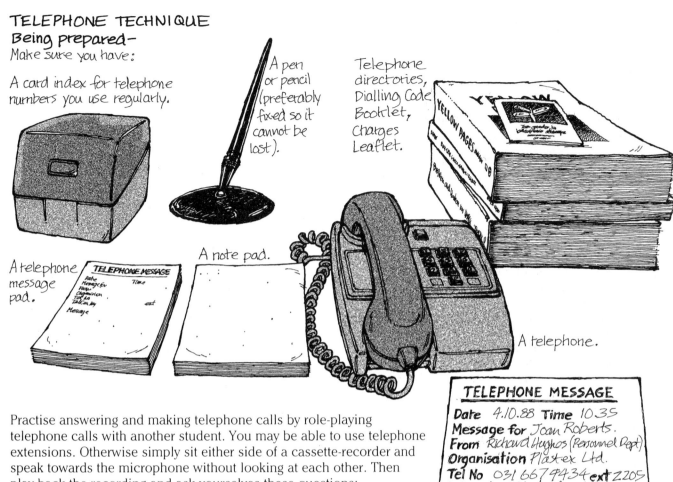

TELEPHONE TECHNIQUE
Being prepared—
Make sure you have:

A card index for telephone numbers you use regularly.

A pen or pencil (preferably fixed so it cannot be lost).

Telephone directories, Dialling Code Booklet, Charges Leaflet.

A telephone message pad.

A note pad.

A telephone.

Practise answering and making telephone calls by role-playing telephone calls with another student. You may be able to use telephone extensions. Otherwise simply sit either side of a cassette-recorder and speak towards the microphone without looking at each other. Then play back the recording and ask yourselves these questions:
Did you *speak clearly*?
Did you sound *interested, courteous and helpful*?
Did you have the *information ready*?
Did you *explain things clearly*?

Answering telephone calls

1. When you answer the phone, give the name of your organisation.
2. If you can deal with the caller's enquiry yourself do so.
3. If you need to fetch someone else to speak to the caller, tell the caller what you are doing. Keep the caller informed of what is happening.
4. If the person the caller wants to speak to is not available, ask the caller whether they would like to leave a message, or would like the person to ring them back.
5. Take down messages on the telephone message form. The form ensures that you write down all the necessary information.

> ### Finding out more
>
> **Telephone services and charges** See telephone directories and leaflets.
> **Equipment** Visit telephone equipment shops and exhibitions on telecommunications. Arrange an educational visit to a telephone exchange.
> **Technique** Visit the switchboard in your own school or college. Watch the telephonist at work.

Making telephone calls

1. Keep costs down. Avoid telephoning in peak charging periods (see telephone charges leaflets), be brief, and do not hang on if the person you want to speak to is not available quickly but call again later instead.
2. Before you call, jot down any notes and information you will need: the name of the person you want to speak to, the questions you want to ask, any dates, facts, etc.
3. When your call is answered, ask for the person or department you want.
4. When you have reached the person or department you need, introduce yourself.
5. Explain clearly what your call is about.

Typing layout and display

If your typing is to look professional you need to know not only how to operate the typewriter but also how to set out your typing on the page so that it looks smart and attractive.

This page suggests a few basic techniques which you will find helpful. After that you simply need to practise and develop an eye for layouts.

Paper

First you need to think about the size and type of paper to use. An A3 piece of paper folded in half produces an A4 size which is the usual size for writing and typing. Folded in half again it becomes an A5 size. You can use paper standing up (called *portrait*) or on its side (*landscape*).

Thick heavy paper is called *bond*, and it is used for *top copies*, eg a business letter. Thin flimsy paper is called *bank*; it is used for the *carbon copy* of the letter which is kept for filing.

Arranging the typing on the paper

1 **Leave plenty of space,** much more than you might think necessary. Have big left and right margins, lots of space at the top and bottom of the page, and plenty of space between paragraphs, titles and headings.

To centre a line of typing

Measure or slightly fold your paper, and make a faint pencil mark at the top to show where the centre line is. Count up the number of letters and spaces in the line of typing. Then, starting from the centre line of your paper, press the backspace key. The number of times you have to press it is half the number of letters and spaces.

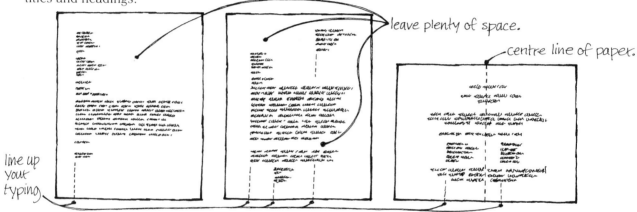

2 **Line up your typing** against a left-hand line, such as the left margin or a tab setting, or *centre* your typing. Try using both techniques in combination.

Different effects

These are useful for making certain parts of your typing stand out. Use them for headings, titles, key paragraphs, and especially for forms and notices.

Capitals
Double-spacing
Underlining
Different line-spacing
Try 1½, 2, or even 3, line-spacing
Ornamental lines
Word processor variables
With a word processor you can vary many other features too. For example, you can alter the size and darkness of the print, and you can *justify* text, ie have straight right-hand margins as well as straight left-hand ones. Make full use of all the variables the word processor offers you.

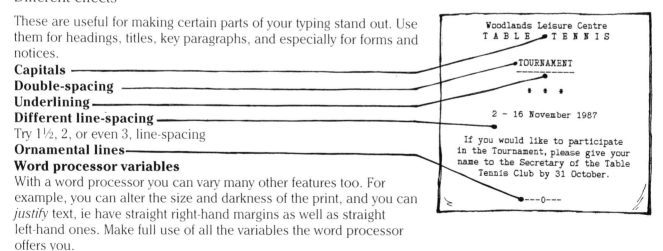

Finding out more

How to develop an eye for layout and design

Collect examples of typing: business letters, advertising circular letters, forms, notices, memos, etc., and especially examples which look smart and attractive. Then study them by going through the entire page pencilling in the effects that have been used.

Touch-typing

Touch-typing is typing with all your fingers, without looking at the keyboard. It is a very fast and satisfying way to type. It is also extremely easy. You can learn the technique in a couple of minutes. After that, it is simply a matter of practice.

If you want to learn quickly, you will need hours of practice every day. An easier way to learn is to do ten minutes' practice every day. If you do this every day without fail, you will be able to touch-type in about six months.

The technique

You simply rest your fingers on the keyboard exactly as shown in the diagram, the fingers of your left hand on the keys *A S D F*, and the fingers of your right hand on the keys *J K L;*. You use those fingers for those keys. To type *G or H*, more your finger across from *F or J*, and then move it back to the resting position.

You treat the keys in the line above and below in exactly the same way. Your left-hand fingers press *Q W E R*, your right-hand fingers press *U I O P*, and you also use your *R* and *U* fingers for *T* and *Y*. When you press keys in the line above or below, try to move only the appropriate finger up or down, keeping the other fingers in the resting position.

Use either thumb to press the space-bar. For capitals, use the little finger of one hand to hold down the shift key while you press the key you want with a finger on the other hand. The other keys are only used occasionally, and you simply look at the keyboard when you want to use them.

It's as simple as that.

Curve your fingers round like this so they are able to hit the keys smartly.

Learning

To learn, you simply have to practise pressing the keys without looking at the keyboard. Look at the page you are copying from, look at the diagram, look at your typing, but do not look at the keyboard.

Step 1 Middle row Begin by typing the letters in the resting position: *asdfg hjkl;*. Do this over and over again until your fingers get used to typing those letters. Then try typing words based on those letters. For example: *ass; all; dad; ask; had; gas; fag;*. Do not look at the keyboard. You have to remember which finger types each letter.

Step 2 Top row Once you have learnt the keys in the middle line of the keyboard, you do exactly the same with the line above, but remember to keep your fingers on the resting position keys, moving only the finger you need up or down. So, type: *qwert yuiop* over and over again. Then try moving up and down from one line of keys to another. For example: *aqa; p; sws lol ded kik frf juj gtg hyh* and so on.

Then try typing simple words and sentences based on those two lines of keys. For example: *It is quite a wet day. Dad got a red fur hat. She quit her lousy work. Get her two grey jugs. Ask for her. The lad led the party. Ask for his greasy pie. The lass led the way. He plays the guitar.* Remember: two spaces after a full stop, question mark, or exclamation mark, and one space after a comma, colon, or semi-colon, etc.

Step 3 Bottom row Similarly, type *zxcub nm,..* Then: *aza sxs l.l dcd, k, fvf mjm gbg hnh*, etc, followed by sentences: *Get all the air you can. The man had six oxo. Ask her for her ice box. We live in View Close. Let us fly our kites. Book a table for Bob. She had a quick visit to the zoo. Get him his old mug. How many apples are there? How did she cut the log? Did you fix the old car?*

From now on, simply practise any piece of typing without looking at the keyboard.

Records department

Records controls the bookings and keeps the membership records. You will receive requests and queries about bookings and membership passed on by Reception and Typing. Some of these requests will be on the appropriate forms, but many will be in telephone messages or letters.

> **What to do**
>
> 1. Create a Membership File and a Membership Number Index as described below.
> 2. Write each booking request and membership application on to the appropriate form if it is not already on a form.
> 3. Process each booking request, as described below.
> 4. Process each membership application, as described below.
> 5. Keep the Membership files up to date, as described below.

Membership files

Make a *Membership File* by filing all the Membership forms together in alphabetical order of the member's name. This will allow you to find out a member's details if you know the member's name.

You will also need a *Membership Number Index* to tell you the member's name if you only know their membership number. You can make a Membership Number Index by simply writing down the numbers in order on a sheet of paper with the name beside each number, or you can use a card-index file, numbering the cards in order, or you could make copies of the Membership forms and file them in number order.

Keep the Membership files up to date. Each day, remove out-of-date memberships from both Membership files. A useful way of doing this is to keep a third Membership file in date order, an *Expiry Date File*. Each day you simply remove the memberships which have expired on that day; these will all be at the front of the file. Store the removed forms in *Out-Of-Date Files*. Remember that membership in each category is limited, as described below. If a category of membership is full, keep a waiting list of applicants who are waiting for membership. You do this by filing those membership forms in date order of application in a *Waiting List File*. If a member has not renewed their membership before the expiry date, then the number becomes available for the next applicant on the waiting list.

There are only a hundred memberships available in each of the four categories of membership.

	Membership Nos
OFF-PEAK Membership	100–199
PEAK Membership	200–299
FAMILY Membership	300–399
CONCESSION Membership	400–499

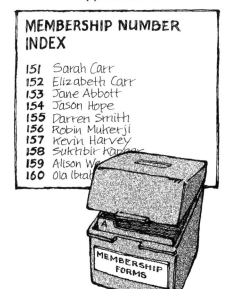

MEMBERSHIP NUMBER INDEX

151 Sarah Carr
152 Elizabeth Carr
153 Jane Abbott
154 Jason Hope
155 Darren Smith
156 Robin Mukerji
157 Kevin Harvey
158 Sukhbir Ka...
159 Alison W...
160 Ola Ibra...

How to process membership applications

If a membership number is available in the category requested:

1. Tick and initial the *Membership Accepted* box on the Membership form.
2. Write in the membership number.
3. Fill in the *Membership Begins* and *Expires* dates.
4. Pass the form to Accounts.

When the form is returned to you from Administration, file it in the Membership Forms File, and make corresponding entries in the Membership Number Index and Expiry Date File.

If a membership number is not available, tick and initial the *Waiting List* box. Then send the form to Administration who will write to inform the applicant and return the Membership form to you for filing in the Waiting List File.

How to process booking requests

Check the booking charts to see if the requested booking is available. If it is, make the booking by writing the member's name in that slot on the booking chart. Then tick and initial the *Booking Accepted* box on the Booking Request form, and pass the Booking Request form to Accounts.

If the requested booking is *not* available, tick and initial the *Booking Not Accepted* box and pass the form on to Administration, who will write to inform the member.

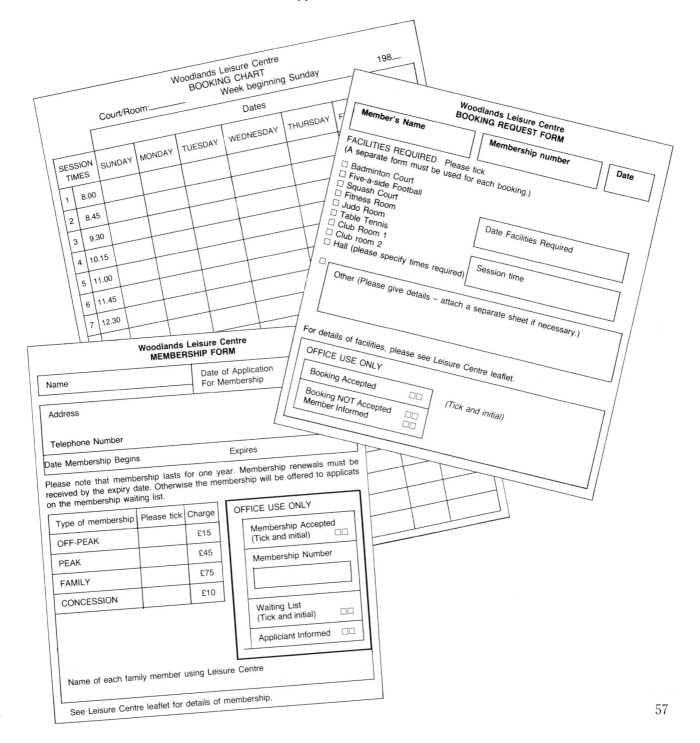

Accounts department

Accounts is responsible for calculating the bills (the *invoices*) which are sent to members. Accounts also deals with queries from customers about their invoices, and checks that the members are paying their bills on time.

Records sends Accounts Membership forms and Booking Request forms which they have processed. These forms provide the information to produce the invoices.

What to do

1. Sort out the Membership and Booking Request forms so that all the forms relating to each member are together.
2. Produce an invoice for each member, as described below.
3. Deal with any queries from members by writing the information asked for on a memo. Then send the memo, with member's letter attached, to Administration, who will write a letter of reply to the member.
4. Deal with overdue invoices by sending the details on a memo to Administration who will write a reminder letter to the member.

The invoice

An invoice is a bill, giving details of what the customer is being charged for, which is posted to the customer. The customer then returns the invoice with the payment. Each organisation designs its own invoices. This is the Leisure Centre's invoice.

Number each invoice you produce. The first invoice is number 1, the second number 2, etc. This helps to identify them in case of any query.

Payment terms This is to encourage the customer to pay the invoice quickly. It means the customer can give themselves a reduction of 5% on the TOTAL shown *if* they pay within 2 days. Otherwise the full (net) amount must be paid.

E&OE Errors and Omissions Excepted means you have the right to change the invoice if you discover you have made a mistake.

```
Woodlands Leisure Centre
2 The Causeway WATERFORD WA19 3AT        Tel: (0988) 45287

Invoice no 24                             Date 2 October 1987

Ms Fiona Savihs
25 Belsize Lane
WATERFORD WA3 5QT                         Terms 5% 2 days
                                                Otherwise net
```

Quantity	Description	Price	Amount
2	Badminton Court Off Peak Bookings (3 Oct. 2:00pm; 4 Oct, 8:00 pm)	£3.00	£6.00
3	Fitness Room Peak Bookings (5 Oct., 12:30pm; 6 Oct 12:30pm and 7 Oct 12:30pm) (35% surcharge)	£1.35	£4.05
1	Fitness Room Off-Peak Booking (7 Oct, 2:00 pm)	£1.00	£1.00
E&OE		TOTAL	£11.05

How to produce leisure centre invoices

For each member, complete an invoice form *in duplicate*, based on the information shown on the Membership and Booking Request forms. The charges for membership and bookings are in the Leisure Centre booklet. Take great care to be accurate in your charges and calculations.

Send the *top* copy of the invoice to Administration, who will send it on to the member with a letter. File the *carbon* copy, with the Membership and Booking Request forms, in date order with the earliest dates at the front of the file. Name the file *Outstanding Invoices*, meaning that they have not been paid.

When you receive payments from the members, write *Paid* on your carbon copy invoice, and put it in a file named *Paid Invoices*. Each day, check the file to see if there are any overdue invoices. These are invoices which have not been paid within two days of the invoice date, and they will always be at the front of the file.

% Percentages

You do not need to know a great deal of maths for business, but you do need to be able to calculate percentages.

Understanding percentages

Per cent just means *out of a hundred*. *Cent* means a *hundred*, as in *century*, *dollars and cents*, *centimetres*.

Imagine a block of wood, sliced into a 100 pieces.

10 per cent would be 10 of the hundred pieces. 50 per cent would be 50 of the 100 pieces, or a half.

In business, there are two types of percentage calculations you need to be able to do:

Calculating a percentage, eg finding out what 5% of something is, as on an invoice.

Expressing something as a percentage, eg the amount of invoices that are overdue for payment.

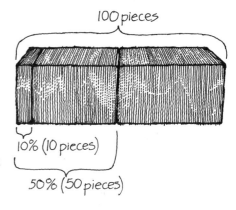

Calculating a percentage

To find 5% of something, divide it into a 100 slices, and then take 5 slices.

So, Fiona Savihs can reduce her invoice by 55p to £10.50 if she pays within 2 days.

in other words

$$\frac{£11\cdot05}{100} \times 5 = £0\cdot5525 \; (i.e. \, 55p)$$

because it is closer to 55p than 56p

Expressing something as a percentage

Suppose that you like to know, from day to day, how many invoices are overdue for payment. It is important to keep an eye on things like this in business. On one day you have 6 out of 24 invoices overdue, on the next day 11 out of 50, and on the day after that 8 out of 40. It is difficult to see if things are getting better or worse. The answer is to express each one as a percentage.

How to express 6 out of 24 as a percentage.

You have a row of invoices, and 6 out of the 24 invoices are overdue.

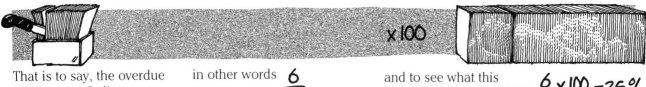

That is to say, the overdue invoices are 6 slices out of a row of 24 slices

in other words $\frac{6}{24}$

and to see what this would look like out of 100 slices you just multiply by 100.

$\frac{6}{24} \times 100 = 25\%$

$\frac{6}{24} \times 100 = 25\%$, $\frac{11}{50} \times 100 = 22\%$, $\frac{8}{40} \times 100 = 20\%$

... so, in fact, things are getting better.

Remember	
To find x% of something	To express a part as a percentage of the total
$\frac{something}{100} \times x =$	$\frac{part}{total} \times 100 =$

Administration department

Administration writes letters dealing with booking and membership matters, and letters in reply to enquiries.

> **What to do**
>
> 1. Design standard letters, as described below, for:
>   - refusal of membership application,
>   - refusal of booking request,
>   - a covering letter for invoices.
>
>   Ask Reception and Typing to produce multiple copies for you to use.
>
> 2. Put the Membership forms in alphabetical order of members' names to make a Membership file. You will need this to look up members' addresses.
>
> 3. Deal with membership and booking forms, invoices and enquiries as described below.

How to deal with membership forms, booking forms, invoices and enquiries

You will receive forms from Records showing membership applications and booking requests which have been refused because they were not available. Deal with these by sending a standard letter to inform the member. The letter must be courteous and regretful in tone. In the case of refused membership, the letter should explain that the person's name has been put on the waiting list and that they will be offered membership as soon as it becomes available.

You will receive invoices from Accounts which need to be sent to members with a short covering letter: use a standard letter for this.

Deal with any enquiries or other letters which the Centre may receive by obtaining the necessary information from the relevant department and writing a letter of reply.

For all letters

Write the letter by hand and give it to Reception and Typing to be typed with a carbon copy. When Reception and Typing return it to you, check and then sign the top copy of the letter. Pass the top copy, with its envelope, back to Reception and Typing for posting. File the carbon copy, in alphabetical order of members' names, in a file marked *Correspondence*.

Some technical terms

Covering letter If you are sending something to someone, for instance, an invoice or a leaflet, it is usual to put a very short letter in the envelope as well, just to explain what you are doing. For example:
I enclose a supply of Booking Request forms as you requested in your telephone call today.

Standard letter This is a letter which you use over and over again for a specific purpose. For example, to remind members that they are late in paying their invoice:
According to our records, we have not yet received payment for your invoice number _____, dated _____. If you have not done so already, please send the payment as soon as possible.
The name, address, invoice number and date have to be changed each time you use the letter. This can be done in handwriting on a typed letter with blanks in it, or by typing out the complete letter each time, or, best of all, by using a word processor (see page 75).

Circular letter This is a letter which is sent to many, perhaps thousands of, people. It is usually used for advertising or making announcements. For example:
For the next month, the Leisure Centre is offering a 10% discount on Monday evening bookings. To be sure of obtaining your booking at this special discount rate, send in your booking requests as soon as possible.
For convenience, circular letters often do not have a date, or the name and address of the person they are being sent to.

Business letters

Business letters should have the following features:

References
Our ref., the Leisure Centre's reference, shows that the copy of this letter is filed under *SILVER*, that the letter was written by Pete Baikie, and typed by Stuart Ainsworth. When Ms Silver writes a letter in reply she will quote the Leisure Centre's reference as *Your ref.*, and this will enable the Leisure Centre staff to match up her letter with this letter.

Ms Silver does not use a reference of her own, so the *Your ref.* is left blank.

Heading
This helps the person receiving the letter to see what it is about.

Body of the letter
Business letters must be *brief*, *clear* and *polite*. Write in a simple, straightforward style, and try not to use flowery, meaningless expressions.

Begin by explaining what you are writing about.

Use a separate paragraph for each point.

Finish with a courteous ending.

If you do not know the person's name, use 'Yours faithfully'.

Letterhead
Business letters are not written on blank paper but on paper which has the organisation's name, address and other information *printed* on it. This is called *headed paper*. This shows that the letter is genuine, and it provides information which the person receiving the letter needs.

```
                    Woodlands Leisure Centre
                    2 The Causeway  WATERFORD WA19 3AT
                         Telephone:  (0988) 45287

Your ref.
Our ref.   SILVER/PB/SA                              6 October 1988

Ms I Silver
42 Granby Road
WATERFORD
WA13 9YF


Dear Ms Silver

AEROBICS CLASS

Thank you for your letter of 5 October 1988, enquiring about
facilities for a weekly Aerobics Class.

I am sure an Aerobics Class would prove popular with our members,
and we would be very pleased to provide you with the facilities.

We have a Judo Room, equipped with exercise mats, which could
accommodate about ten people.  Alternatively, you could hire the
Hall which would be suitable for a very large group.  The Hall is
also equipped with mats.

I have enclosed a leaflet which gives full details of membership
and bookings, together with membership and booking forms.

We look forward to hearing from you.

Yours sincerely



Pete Baikie
Administration Department

enc.  Leisure Centre Leaflet
      Membership Application Form
      Booking Request Form
```

Your signature
Your name and title or department

Enclosure
Enc. tells the person receiving the letter that there is something enclosed with the letter in the envelope.

Date

Name and address of the person the letter is being sent to.
This is put on the letter so that it will appear on the carbon copy of the letter. Otherwise you would not know whom you had sent the letter to.

If you are writing to someone in another organisation, you should also include their title, eg *Sales Manager*, and/or their department, eg *Sporting Equipment Section*, and the organisation's name, eg *Thoroughbred Supplies Ltd*.

Always use the person's name if you know it. Otherwise write *Dear Madam/Sir*. In a circular letter you can write *Dear Member*, etc.

Assessment profile

This profile helps you assess what you have learnt in this activity. You should aim to have achieved at least Level 2 in every section, and Level 3 in most sections. Work with a colleague to fill in the profile, making sure you can convince your colleague that you have achieved each level. Tick each level that you have achieved.

	Level 1	**Level 2**	**Level 3**	**Level 4**
Organisational Structure	Can explain some jobs each Department does.	Can explain what each Department does.	Can explain how each Department's work connects with other Departments.	Can explain reasons for each Department's share of work.
Reception Dept Mail procedures	Can explain some mail procedures.	Can list all steps of mail procedures correctly and in order.	Have had some practice in handling mail.	Have handled in-coming and outgoing mail quickly and correctly.
Reception Dept Telephone technique	Can list the items which need to be kept beside the telephone.	Can explain, in detail and correctly, how to deal with incoming and outgoing calls.	Have demonstrated this technique in practice.	Have found out more. (as described on page 53)
Reception Dept Typing	Have produced some simple typing layouts.	Have experimented and designed own typing layouts.	Can demonstrate principles of touch-typing.	Have practised touch-typing Steps 1–3 (on page 55).
Records Dept Record-keeping	Can fill out Membership and Booking forms correctly.	Can describe the records which the Department keeps.	Have some experience of using forms and keeping records in the Records Department.	Can demonstrate how to keep files up to date.
Accounts Dept Invoices	Can give simple explanation of what an invoice is.	Can describe and explain all the features of an invoice.	Can describe exactly how to produce invoices, and how to keep the associated records.	Have produced many correct invoices, and kept the associated records correctly.
Accounts Dept Percentages	Can explain what per cent means.	Can confidently explain how to calculate a percentage of an amount.	Can confidently explain how to express an amount as a percentage.	Have numerous examples of correctly calculated percentages in your own work.
Administration Dept Business letters	Can describe some features of a business letter.	Can identify and explain all the features of a given business letter.	Can correctly set out business letters without using notes or textbook.	Have produced acceptable business letters without notes, and can describe different types of business letters.

Date completed _____   Signed _____

Events

Now that you have had some practice in operating your organisation you are ready to use it for real administrative and commercial ventures. The best way to begin is to undertake some administrative jobs within your own school or college.

Perhaps the most obvious administrative venture is to organise events, such as Open Days, Parents Evenings, Christmas parties and discos.

SHOULD YOU MAKE MONEY?

Should you aim to make a profit out of organising events, or should you organise them free of charge? If you do make a profit, should you spend the money on yourselves or donate the money to some other use? These are important decisions which you will need to discuss with your school or college.

Main issues

What is your motivation? Are you only interested in making money or do you also enjoy helping people?

As the Standard of Living Game showed (pages 11–15), businesses can be set up either to make money (private sector organisations set up and owned by private individuals) or to meet a need (public sector organisations set up by the government for the public). Making money is exciting, but operating an organisation and providing a service for people can be satisfying activities in themselves.

Is it right to make money? Are you entitled to? Is it fair? Are you really earning the money, or has some of it been produced by others? Remember that you are using accommodation, heating, facilities and teaching help (the **Capital**) provided by your school or college, as well as your own work (your **Labour**).

However, the same problem applies to all organisations today. All organisations use the Capital (land, buildings, equipment, money) created by others. The question is: who should get the benefits?

Does it help you learn? Would the excitement of making money help you to work harder and learn more?

Everyone needs an incentive, and it is only fair that you should be rewarded for your work. On the other hand, money need not be the only incentive. Perhaps your reward is the education you receive, but that may not seem a very exciting reward.

There is no simple answer to the question of whether you should make money out of organising events. You will need to consider all these issues and balance different points of view.

> *For details of how to raise money to start your ventures, see page 70.*
> For further information see *Outline of the Economy* and *Types of Business and Administration Organisations* (pages 112–120).

How to organise events

Stage 1	*Thinking* about what event or activity to organise. Each Department needs to think up ideas, and decide who is going to present them at the meeting.
Stage 2	*Meeting* to discuss ideas. The meeting needs to decide what events or activities should be organised. Then it needs to draw up an action plan.
Stage 3	*Obtaining information* about: Approvals and permission for the event or activity. How the event should be arranged, eg discussions with the school or college about what is required for an Open Day. What rooms and equipment would be needed and would be available. Costs of goods and services required, eg cost of coffee and biscuits for a Parents Evening; cost of a DJ for a disco. Calculations of how much money is needed, and how much to charge to cover costs. What arrangements need to be made, eg for appropriate staff to be available at an employers' reception, what signs and notices would be needed.
Stage 4	*Meeting* to decide on how to organise the event. This may take several meetings. Now that the information has been obtained, the meeting needs to agree on an action plan about how the event will be organised and who will do what.
Stage 5	*Organising the event* This includes notifying the people and organisations involved about what will be happening, booking rooms and equipment, buying or ordering goods and services, publicising the event*, preparing signs and notices, and arranging for the necessary people to be present. *See page 84 for suggestions on publicity.*
Stage 6	*The event* This involves arranging rooms and setting up equipment and facilities, running the event, clearing up afterwards, returning equipment, and paying the bills.
Stage 7	*Review meeting* This meeting discusses whether the event was successful, what the financial position is, and what conclusions can be drawn, especially if your organisation is to organise more events.

Types of events and other administrative work

Open days Parents evenings. College receptions for local employers.

Shows and exhibitions Theatrical and musical productions. Displays and exhibitions of students' work, eg fashion shows produced by fashion students.

Parties and discos Christmas parties, regular discos, end-of-year celebrations, live bands.

Sports and societies Organising occasional or regular sporting events in the gym or common room. Helping clubs and societies in your school or college with administrative work.

Student Union work Providing administrative support, eg organising meetings, producing and circulating leaflets, helping with Student Union sales.

Administrative support to school/college Eg, mail-shots for Parent-Teacher Association, handling sales of stationery and new or second-hand textbooks.

Other ventures Try advertising the administrative services you can offer. Publicise your services not only in your school or college but also amongst local community groups and organisations.

What each department does

	Reception	Records	Accounts	Administration
Stage 1			Think up ideas.	Prepares agenda for meeting.
Stage 2	A Reception person chairs meeting.	MEETING		Takes minutes of meeting.
Stage 3	Information-gathering tasks distributed amongst different departments according to departmental expertise, eg: Verbal information-gathering (telephone calls and talking to people in person). Keeps written records of all discussions. Typing.	Keeps a record of whether the action plan is being followed. Collects and combines the information gathered by other departments.	Obtains financial information, ie costs, prices. Calculates likely expenditure, income and profits/surplus.	Writes and circulates minutes of meeting. Writes letters requesting information; sends off for information leaflets. Prepares agenda.
Stage 4	A Reception person chairs meeting.	MEETING		Takes minutes of meeting.
Stage 5	Makes arrangements by speaking to people in person and on the telephone.	Co-ordinates arrangements made by each department. Stock control, eg of tickets, drinks.	Handles purchases, book-keeping, bank account and cash.	Circulates minutes. Writes letters. Publicity materials. Signs and notices.
Stage 6	Reception duties and sales.	Stock control.	Handles money and bills.	Overall co-ordination of event.
Stage 7	A Reception person chairs meeting.	MEETING	Presents receipts and payment account.	Takes minutes of meeting.

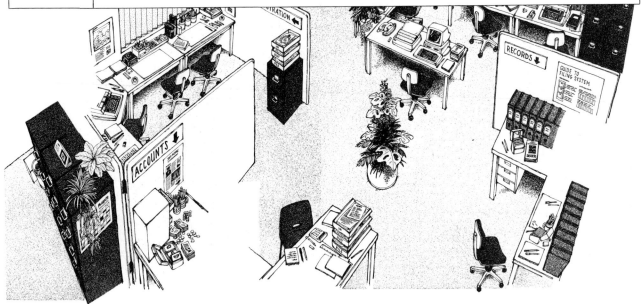

Business meetings

A business meeting enables people to discuss matters and reach decisions in a properly organised way.

How to hold business meetings

1 The notice of meeting

First of all you have to notify people that there will be a meeting. You can do this by letter or memo or by a notice on a notice-board.

```
                    INSTANT ADMIN
                  Notice of Meeting

The next meeting to discuss the organising of events will be held
on Friday 13 November at 2.00pm in Room 211.

Please submit agenda items to Robert, the Minutes Secretary, by
12 November.
```

2 The agenda

Then you need to draw up an *agenda*, that is, a list of the topics which will be discussed at the meeting.

The agenda can be sent out in advance, perhaps with the notice of the meeting, or it can be given to people at the beginning of the meeting.

The first three items and the last two items on an agenda are always the same. The items in between are what the meeting is really about.

Each member of the meeting has a copy of the agenda and the minutes of the previous meeting.

Finding out more

To find out more about meetings visit some meetings in your school, college, town hall and community groups. Look at the agenda and minutes and notice the procedure used at the meeting.

3 The meeting itself

The Chair introduces each agenda item, and invites the members of the meeting to discuss it.

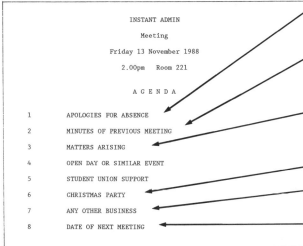

An announcement about who is not able to attend the meeting.

The meeting decides whether the minutes of the previous meeting are correct. (See next page.)

A chance to discuss anything arising from the previous meeting that is not dealt with elsewhere in the agenda. These are usually small items, such as the latest news or developments of matters discussed at the previous meeting.

The main part of the meeting.

A chance for people to discuss other matters which are not on the agenda.

A quick discussion to agree on when to meet again.

The Chair or Chairperson is the person who conducts the meeting. The Chair must ensure that the discussion keeps to the point, and that everyone has a chance to speak. The Chair must also try to guide the discussion towards an agreed decision. If the meeting cannot agree then the Chair can put the matter to a vote.

Chairing a meeting is a skilful task which requires great tact and an ability to remain calm. The person must be able to follow the debate, sum up the points made, and propose a decision.

The Minutes secretary takes the minutes of the meeting. They make notes on what is decided at the meeting, and then write the minutes based on these notes.

4 The minutes

The minutes are the written record of the meeting. They are important because they show what was decided at the meeting and who said they would do what. This means that minutes can be used to find out what should be happening and who should be carrying out which tasks. Because they have this importance, the minutes have to be approved as a correct record at the next meeting.

INSTANT ADMIN
M I N U T E S
of meeting held on
Friday 13 November 1988 2.00pm Room 211

1. APOLOGIES FOR ABSENCE
   Sarah was unable to attend because she was ill.

2. MINUTES OF PREVIOUS MEETING (Held Monday 9 November 1988)
   The minutes were accepted as a correct record of the previous meeting.

3. MATTERS ARISING

   Regarding item 5 in Minutes of 9 November: the date for the Fashion students' next Fashion Show had not yet been decided. The Fashion Course Tutor would contact Instant Admin when a date had been fixed to discuss help in organising the event.

4. OPEN DAY OR SIMILAR EVENT
   Anna and Sanjay had made an appointment to see the Head of Business Studies about this. They would report back to the next meeting.

5. STUDENT UNION SUPPORT
   The Students Union would like help with sales of SU T-shirts and literature, and with organising the next SU elections. The SU President would come to the next meeting to explain further.

6. CHRISTMAS PARTY
   Each department reported on the information it had obtained. It was decided that the Christmas Party would be for all students and staff of the Business Studies Department, and would be held on Friday 11 December at 6.00pm. Tickets would be £2.50.
   The following action plan was agreed.

   - Samantha, Varsha and Nadia would book the Hall and the necessary equipment.
   - The Administration Department would produce publicity materials in draft form for discussion at the next meeting.
   - Robert, Peter and Wayne would buy the decorations and decorate the Hall by 9 December.
   - The Accounts Department would produce a more detailed budget for food and drink for discussion at the next meeting.
   - Michael would ask the Caretaker about using the stage lighting for the party.
   - Sharon would book the DJ, and the DJ's light show if the stage lighting was not available.

7. ANY OTHER BUSINESS
   It was agreed that a Get Well card be sent to Sarah since she had now been ill for two weeks. Varsha would buy the card and circulate it for everyone to sign.

8. DATE OF NEXT MEETING
   Wednesday 18 November at 10.30am in Room 211

The minutes are set out exactly like the agenda, but with a short statement about what was decided under each item.

Costing and pricing

In organising events, as in any other venture, you need to work out how much the event is going to cost and what price to charge for it.

Costing

Suppose you expect about 100 people to come to your Christmas Party. You work out the costs as follows.

Item		Cost £
Food (snacks)		27.00
Drinks		105.00
Hire of glasses, plates		5.00
Decorations		18.00
DJ & light show		62.00
Stationery		8.00
Photocopying		5.00
	Costs	£230.00

The party will include a raffle which is expected to provide a revenue, ie an income, of about £10.

The cost of the party will therefore be:

		Costs	230.00
	less	Revenue	− 10.00
		Net Cost	£220.00

So the cost of producing the party will be £220.00 ÷ 100 = £2.20 per person.

Pricing

In deciding what price to charge you have to consider:
 a *Covering your costs* If you are to *break even*, ie not make a profit or a loss, you must charge each customer the cost price: £2.20, *assuming that you will sell all 100 tickets*.
 b *Market forces* You have to judge what people would be willing to pay. If you set the price too low, people might buy tickets and re-sell them at a higher price (the profit thus going to them). If you set the price too high, not all the tickets will be sold, and you might not break even.

Suppose you decide to set the price at £2.50.

Sales: 100 tickets at £2.50 each		£250.00
less *Cost of Sales*		− £220.00
	Profit/surplus	£ 30.00

This also means you reach your break-even point when you have sold 88 tickets.

A graph will show you at a glance the effect of different ticket prices.

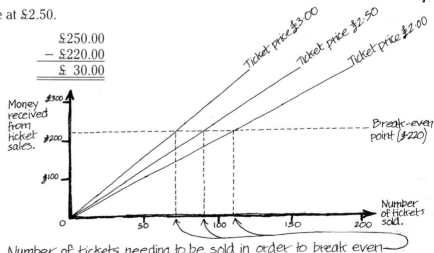

Number of tickets needing to be sold in order to break even

Money and banking

Where to get money to start your venture

You may be able to organise some types of event and undertake some administrative activities without needing any money. However, many other events, such as parties and discos, will require money. How you obtain this money will depend on whether you are operating your organisation as a money-making venture or simply as an administrative unit which carries out work on behalf of others.

Operating as a profit-making venture

If you are operating as a money-making venture, you try to make sufficient profit from each event to provide the money you need to organise more events, and to give you some money for yourselves. This requires skill, efficiency and good business judgement. It also requires daring because your ventures may fail and you could be left with debts.

The money you need to start with is called *Capital* because it is money for the equipment and materials you need. There are three ways of raising your capital:

A Grant Your school or college, or perhaps even some sympathetic local organisation might give you a small amount of money as an outright gift to start you off. This is equivalent to someone starting a business with money inherited from their family.

A Loan Many businesses are started with a bank loan. However a bank requires some security. For example, people offer their house or car as a security, so that if they cannot repay the loan the bank can take the house or car. Since you will not be able to offer any security you will not be able to obtain a bank loan, but you may be able to obtain a small loan from your school or college.

Legal aspects: liability and trading names

You might be tempted to organise, say a Christmas party, by hoping that you will sell enough tickets to be able to pay the DJ at the end of the party. However, if you do not sell enough tickets you will be *liable*, ie responsible, for the debts to the DJ. So, be very careful not to incur any debts you will not be able to pay. This is why you need some initial capital, or a guarantee from your school or college that they will pay any outstanding debts.

If people trade as a company they avoid this problem (see page 119). But you are not a company. You trade as yourselves, as individual people. For this reason, the law (the Companies Act 1981) requires that if you use your organisation name, eg 'INSTANT ADMIN', you must *also* put all your personal names on all business documents.

Shares The easiest way to raise your initial capital may be for each of you to contribute a share of the money needed, perhaps £1 per person. Your incentive for doing this would be that you would also have a share in the profits as well as being able to take back your £1 once the business had established itself. This is how a company operates, although, of course, you would not have *limited liability*.

Draw up a written agreement of how the profits are to be divided between the people who have contributed the share capital.

Operating as an administrative unit

If you are carrying out administrative tasks for others, such as the Student Union, then they would provide the money needed for each event. This is how public sector organisations, such as hospitals, operate. However, it is important to operate with as much skill and efficiency as if you were a money-making venture, so as to provide as good an administrative service as possible and make the best use of people's money.

Operating as a self-financing administrative unit

This means that you function like a money-making organisation, but simply make enough profits to continue in operation. Whatever profits you make do not go into your pockets but into organising future events. This is how nationalised industries, such as British Rail, operate.

For further information see
organisations in the British economy, page 119.

How banks work

Banks keep your money safe, but they are also able to use your money. If you are not using your money, then someone else can use it; they can use the buildings, equipment and goods that it stands for. They can make wealth out of using those things, so they give some of the wealth to you in the form of money. This is called the *interest* on the loan.

Bank accounts

A bank account keeps your money safe. In addition, it will also provide you with interest, or convenient ways of paying bills, depending on the type of account it is. There are two main types of bank accounts:

Deposit accounts are for money that you want to save, rather than use for day-to-day spending. The bank pays you *interest* for keeping your money in a deposit account.

Current accounts are for money that you want to use for day-to-day spending. *Current* means *in use now*. Instead of paying you interest, the bank gives you convenient ways of using the money.

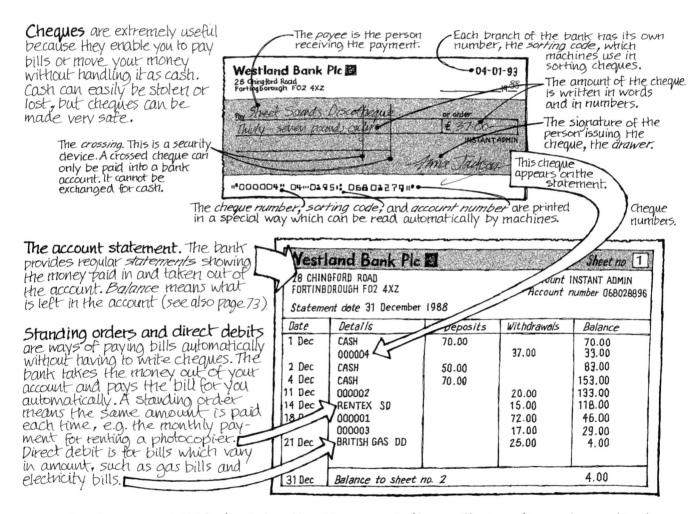

Personal customers, i.e. individual people rather than organisations, with current accounts are also given:

Accounts

Analysed cash book, bank account, receipts and payments account

Handling the money
In organising events you will be taking in money from ticket sales and paying out money for purchases. You will be handling reasonably large amounts of money so you will need a bank account as well as a cash-box.

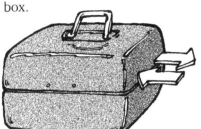

Keep only a small amount of money in the cash-box, say about £25. Put any extra money in the bank account. If you run short of money in the cash-box, take some money out of the bank account and put it into the cash-box. Pay small bills by cash from the cash-box. Pay large bills by cheque.

The analysed cash-book

You will need to keep a record of the money in the cash-box. The way to do this is to use the analysed cash-book.

This is simply an extension of the petty cash-book explained on page 46. It has analysis columns for the money received as well as for the money spent. This gives you a complete picture of where your cash has come from and where it has gone.

	Money **INTO** Cash-Box							Money Taken **OUT** of Cash-Box						
DATE	DETAILS	TOTAL	ANALYSIS				DATE	DETAILS	TOTAL	ANALYSIS				
			Tickets	Raffle	Bank	Misc.				Food	Drink	Decorations	Bank	Misc.
1 Dec	Cash from Bank	50.00			50.00		1 Dec	D.J. Deposit	25.00					25.00
2 Dec	Sales	58.25	57.50	0.75			2 Dec	Stationery	8.00					8.00
								Bank	50.00				50.00	
4 Dec	Sales	85.75	82.50	3.25			4 Dec	Decorations	10.77			10.77		
								Photocopying	5.00					5.00
								Bank	70.00				70.00	
8 Dec	Sales	60.00	60.00				8 Dec	Drinks	33.00		33.00			
								Decorations	7.23			7.23		
								Hire	5.00					5.00
11 Dec	Sales	69.25	45.00	4.25	20.00		11 Dec	Food	27.00	27.00				
							14 Dec	Bank	70.00				70.00	
									311.00	27.00	33.00	18.00	190.00	43.00
								Balance b/d	12.25					
		323.25	245.00	8.25	70.00				323.25					
15 Dec	Balance b/d	12.25												

Whenever you put money *into* the cash-box, enter into the accounts:
• the date,
• the details (where the money has come from),
• the amount in the TOTAL column,
• the amount in the appropriate ANALYSIS column; this will enable you to analyse where money has come from.

When you put money into the bank or take it out of the bank, enter 'Bank' in the DETAILS column.

Similarly, whenever you take money *out* of the cash-box, enter the date, the details, and enter the amount in the TOTAL column and in the appropriate ANALYSIS column.

Balance the cash-book as described on page 47. Remember that the balance is the difference between the money put into the cash-box and the money taken out. Write in this amount to make the two sides of the book balance, ie equal. Then carry the amount down to the INTO side of the book, to show that this is the amount of money still in the box.

Bank account

You will also need to keep a record of money going in and out of your bank account. The easiest way to do this is to keep a record exactly like the bank statement (see page 71). When you receive your bank statement at the end of the month you will then be able to check your record against the bank's record. But remember that it may take several days, even weeks, for a cheque to reach your bank, so dates on the bank statement show the date that your cheques reached the bank, not the date on which they were written.

BANK ACCOUNT				
Date	Details	Deposits	Withdrawals	Balance
1 Dec	CASH (SU loan)	70.00		70.00
	000001 Cash		50.00	20.00
2 Dec	CASH	50.00		70.00
4 Dec	CASH	70.00		140.00
11 Dec	000002 Cash		20.00	120.00
	000003 Drinks		72.00	48.00
	000004 DJ		37.00	11.00
14 Dec	CASH	70.00		81.00
15 Dec	000005 (Return of loan)		70.00	11.00

Compare this record of the bank account with the bank statement on page 71.

Your *analysed cash-book* and your *bank account* show what has happened to the money, but when the event you have organised is over you will need to make an overall summary of how much money you have received and spent to see if you have made a profit (or surplus). This overall summary is called the receipts and payments account.

Receipts and payments account

This account combines the information from the analysed cash-book and the bank account.

The profit (or surplus) is the balance, the difference between the money you have received and the money you have paid out.

RECEIPTS & PAYMENT ACCOUNT					
RECEIPTS	£	PAYMENTS	Cash	Cheques	Total
Ticket sales	245.00	Food (snacks)	27.00		27.00
Raffle	8.25	Drinks	33.00	72.00	105.00
		Hire (glasses etc)	5.00		5.00
		Decorations	18.00		18.00
		DJ & light show	25.00	37.00	62.00
		Stationery	8.00		8.00
		Photocopying	5.00		5.00
			121.00	109.00	230.00
		Balance c/d			23.25
	253.25				253.25
Balance b/d	23.25				

These analysis columns are not essential, but they help you to collect the information about what payments have been made. Eg, see how the Drinks information has been collected: £33 from the *analysed cash-book* (the Drinks column total), and £72 (cheque 000003) from the *bank account*, making an overall total of £105.00. You could also have similar analysis columns for the RECEIPTS if they were needed.

73

Information technology in business

A great deal of business and office work is processing information. For example, filing, keeping records and accounts, and sending information by telephone and mail. It is now possible for much of this work to be done by computers, especially if they are connected together by telephone lines. The name for this is *Information Technology*, or *IT*.

The Computer

The computer is a machine which processes information. The instructions which the computer needs to process the information are called the *program* or the *software*. The machinery is called the *hardware*. To use a computer, you first *load* the software into the computer, and then enter the information which the computer processes. When you have finished, you store (*save*) the processed information on a magnetic disk.

The **minicomputer** is a medium-sized computer, which fills a small room. It can hold all the information needed for a company. It can be used by many people throughout the building. Each person has a *terminal* (a monitor and keyboard).

The **mainframe computer** is a very big computer which fills several rooms. It holds huge amounts of information and can be used by anyone around the world who can link their own computer to the mainframe computer through telephone lines.

The **microcomputer** is a small computer for just one person. It is small enough to fit on a desk top.

MONITOR or VDU (Visual Display Unit)
This screen shows you what is happening: what information is being entered and how it is being processed.

CPU
The Central Processing Unit is the brain of the computer. It is a set of tiny electronic circuits called *silicon chips* or *microprocessors*. They hold the information and process it. However, they cannot hold the information when the machine is switched off, so the information must be stored on the magnetic disks.

DISK DRIVES
The magnetic disks which contain the software and the stored information are put into the computer here.

PRINTER
The printer prints out the processed information. This could be letters, diagrams, charts, accounts, lists, etc.

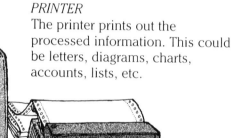

KEYBOARD
This is like a typewriter keyboard. It is used for entering information into the computer and for controlling the computer.

MOUSE
This is another way of controlling the computer in addition to the keyboard. Moving the mouse on the desk top moves an arrow on the screen. When the arrow is pointing at the instruction you want, you press the button on the mouse.

Software

Computers can be used to process different types of information depending on the instructions, the software, which are loaded into the computer. These are the main types of business software.

Word processing   Using the computer as a typewriter.
Data bases   Filing information.
Spread-sheets   Calculations.
Accounting packages   Keeping book-keeping accounts.
Stock control packages   Computerised stock control.
Payroll packages   Working out wages.
Viewdata systems   Up-to-the-minute information provided on computer screens, eg PRESTEL.
Electronic mail   Sending mail (letters, documents, pictures) from one computer to another along telephone lines.

Word processing

Word processing is using the computer as a typewriter. You type your document, eg a letter, onto the monitor screen. You can then correct it and adjust the layout before printing it.

Typing can be stored on the disk. This means that standard letters and documents can be produced very easily by calling them up to the screen, making any alterations and then printing them out. Standard paragraphs can be stored and used in the same way.

Type your letter onto the screen.

You can then adjust the typing as you want...

change any spellings and wording...

move whole paragraphs around...

add in a standard paragraph stored on the disk...

... then print out your finished typing, and save it on the disk for future use.

Print size and style can be varied. You may also be able to include graphs, charts and diagrams.

Example Using a word processing *mailmerge* programme to organise an event. This automatically prints out many copies of a letter, each one individually addressed to a different person.

1 Type in letter.

2 Type in list of names and addresses.
Mailing List:
 A. Andrews, 12 Broad Street.
 R. Coates, 87 Grand Avenue.
 S. Gupta, 12 Appleby Drive.
 G. Patel, 33 Manor Gardens.
 H. Rogers, 11 Tudor Close.
 D. Sahni, 55 Fortress Road.

3 Print out letters individually addressed.

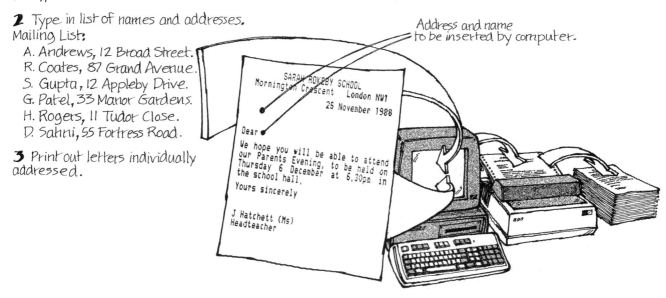

Address and name to be inserted by computer.

Assessment profile

This profile helps you assess what you have learnt in this activity. You should aim to have achieved at least Level 2 in every section, and Level 3 in most sections. Work with a colleague to fill in the profile, making sure you can convince your colleague that you have achieved each level. Tick each level that you have achieved.

	Level 1	**Level 2**	**Level 3**	**Level 4**
All Departments Types of business organisations	Can give some examples of different types of business organisations.	Can explain the difference between private sector and public sector.	Can list the main types of organisation in the private and public sectors.	Can explain and discuss the different purposes and motivations of the different types of organisations.
Administration Dept Business meetings	Can describe some features of business meetings.	Can describe documents and procedures of business meetings.	Have produced notice, agenda and minutes for a meeting.	Have chaired a business meeting.
Accounts Dept Banking	Can explain purpose of bank accounts.	Can explain all the features of cheques and bank statements.	Can describe features of deposit and current accounts.	Can explain how banks operate.
Accounts Dept Costing and pricing	Can explain what is meant by 'costing' and 'pricing'.	Can describe all the steps of costing and pricing a commodity.	Have correctly costed and priced a commodity.	Have produced a graph to show the effects of different pricings.
Accounts Dept Accounts — Analysed Cash-Book, Bank Account, Receipts and Payments Account	Can explain how the money should be handled, and the purpose of the cash-box and bank account.	Can explain how to make entries in the three different accounts and to balance each account.	Can show how the Receipts and Payments Account is produced from the other two accounts, and how the Bank Account is checked against the bank statement.	Have produced a complete set of correct accounts.
Reception Dept Information technology in business	Can explain what 'IT' means and what a computer is.	Can describe different sizes of computers.	Can identify and explain the different parts of a computer system.	Can describe and give examples of software.
Reception Dept IT: word processing	Can explain what 'word processing' means.	Can describe main features of word processing.	Have used a word processing package on a computer.	Can demonstrate on a computer all the main operations of word processing.

Date completed _____   Signed _____

Student travel agency

You can use your administrative organisation to operate a student travel agency. You organise outings and day trips, even weekend or week-long trips abroad, for yourselves and for others. Your organisation has to devise the ideas, do the research, costings and marketing, design the package, publicise and promote it, handle money and bookings, and finally manage the actual trip itself.

Finding out more about travel agencies

Visit a travel agency. Find out about the market research they do, where they get reference information, how they make bookings, and how they operate in general.

How to operate a student travel agency

Stage 1	*Thinking up possible trips* The meeting needs to discuss suggestions and then draw up a detailed action plan showing which departments will gather what information by when, ie Stages 2–4.
Stage 2	*Preliminary rough information* Finding out what trips are possible, and roughly how much they would cost. Consult travel agents, timetables and enquiry offices, library, PRESTEL, and find out if the school or college minibus could be used.
Stage 3	*Market research* Finding out whether people would be interested in the trips you have thought up, what price they would be willing to pay, and what similar packages are offered elsewhere.
Stage 4	*Deciding what trip or package deal to create* The meeting would base this decision on the results of Stage 3, and also decide on the price. An action plan covering Stages 5–9 is agreed.
Stage 5	*Getting detailed information* Getting exact information *in writing* about forms and costs of transport, admission prices, meals, activities and general information.
Stage 6	*Designing trip or package in detail* This includes negotiating discounts, grants, sponsorship and group rates.
Stage 7	*Publicity* including leaflets, posters, announcements in tutorials, etc. *Making tickets* Producing an *information sheet* for those going on the trip.
Stage 8	*Selling tickets & making bookings* This includes paying deposits, selling tickets, keeping accounts, stock control of tickets, and payments.
Stage 9	*Managing the trip itself* Making sure the trip is successful by ensuring all the arrangements operate smoothly.

These are the stages needed for each trip or package deal. You can of course organise several different trips or package deals at the same time.

Trips you could organise

These are the sort of trips and outings you could arrange.

Purely for pleasure
Day and weekend trips to
- The seaside, eg Blackpool.
- Theme park, eg Alton Towers, or a safari park.
- Abroad, eg Boulogne in France.
- Famous places, eg Stonehenge, London.
- The countryside, eg the Lake District.
- Historic places, eg castles, palaces.
- Fun-fairs and restaurants.

Educational visits
These can be interesting, and are often free:
- Unusual places that you would normally never get the chance to see, eg a chocolate factory.
- Glamorous places, eg TV or recording studios, backstage at the theatre, the Houses of Parliament.
- Exhibitions and museums. Many large organisations and most museums mount free exhibitions which can be surprisingly interesting.

Also
- Theatre and cinema trips. These will be of particular interest to literature students.
- Outdoor activities, eg skiing, rambling, sailing. You can arrange weekend accommodation in youth hostels. See what facilities and help your local education authority can provide; they often have hostels and equipment.

What each department does

	Reception	Records	Accounts	Administration
Stage 1	A Reception person chairs meeting.	MEETING		Takes minutes of meeting.
Stage 2	Verbal information-gathering: telephone calls and visits to travel agents, etc.	Keeps a record of names and addresses contacted and of action plan progress. Files information.	Obtains financial information: costs, prices, etc.	Writes up and circulates minutes of meeting. Written enquiries and letters.
Stages 3	Types and uses questionnaire, types Market Research Report.	Records issue and returns of questionnaires.	Analyses questionnaire results; % in favour, bar charts, etc.	Devises questionnaire and writes Market Research Report.
Stage 4	A Reception person chairs meeting.	MEETING	Explains analysis of questionnaire results.	Explains Report's recommendations. Takes minutes.
Stage 5	Visits to travel agents for printed/written details.	Progress of action plan. Files information.	Obtains financial information: costs, prices, etc.	Writes up and circulates minutes. Writes letters.
Stage 6	Negotiates discounts. Typing.	Records exact details of package.	Exact costings and pricing.	Writes letters.
Stage 7	Typing and reprographics.	Records publicity actions. Leaflets. Stock control.	Book-keeping: spending on stationery and materials.	Designs publicity and information sheet.
Stage 8	Sells tickets. Deals with enquiries from students/customers.	Stock control of tickets, information sheets. Filing.	Book-keeping. Handles money. Makes payments.	Fills out booking forms. Writes letters of confirmation.
Stage 9	Provides information. Answers queries.	Checks everyone is present and keeps to timetable.	Pays bills. Collects receipts.	Issues travel pills, vouchers, etc.

Put together a package at one inclusive price

For example:
Trip to London *plus* floating disco on Thames
Riverboat ride *plus* TV studios visit
Theatre visit *plus* interval drinks *plus* chocolates *plus* programme *plus* café supper
Day trip to Boulogne *plus* lunch in real French restaurant *plus* tour of old town

Negotiate a good deal
Make sure you get full benefit of group rates and discounts. Find out what is provided free or paid for by the local authority, Government, or EEC as a service. For example, the EEC provides generous subsidies for educational visits to the EEC institutions at Brussels and Strasbourg.

Profit or service to community?

When thinking about what trips to organise, bear in mind that not everyone has the money to pay for trips and outings. Don't limit your interest and activities to those which will make profits for your organisation. Use your organisation to provide a service for those who need it. Try to make use of reduced rates and local authority money for students, local pensioners, the disabled or single-parent families. Negotiate special rates, help from charities, commercial sponsorship. Organise trips for teachers and parents too, or for local community groups.

Market research

Before you go to the trouble and expense of organising a trip you must find out whether it is likely to sell. Finding out whether there is a market, that is, whether there are likely to be customers for a particular product, is called *market research*, and it is usually conducted by means of a questionnaire.

Designing a questionnaire

Identify the target group. Here it is ALL students. If you think that some trips would be of more interest to some students than others, then you would need to include questions identifying the type of student and course.

State the purpose of the questionnaire as exactly as possible. This helps you get the co-operation of the people who answer the questionnaire, the *respondents*. It also helps you to choose questions which will produce the information you need. Avoid irrelevant questions. For example, the name of the respondent is not relevant in this questionnaire.

You can use different types of questions: YES/NO questions, category questions, etc.

However, be careful of open-ended questions which just give the respondent a blank box. The answers can be difficult to summarise in your report.

MARKET RESEARCH
QUESTIONNAIRE TO ALL STUDENTS

This questionnaire is intended to find out whether students would be interested in trips and outings organised by the student business organisation INSTANT ADMIN.

1. Which of the following trips would you be interested in? (*Please tick appropriate boxes.*)
   - ☐ Seaside
   - ☐ France (Boulogne)
   - ☐ Safari Park
   - ☐ Castle/Palace
   - ☐ Stonehenge
   - ☐ Nuclear Power-Station
   - ☐ Technology Exhibition on Satellite TV
   - ☐ Fashion Exhibition: Fashion 1980–2000
   - ☐ London
   - ☐ Theatre
   - ☐ Lake District
   - ☐ Rock-climbing
   - ☐ Restaurant
   - ☐ Cinema

2. What length of trip would you be *most* interested in?
   (*Please indicate your order of preference by putting 1 in your first choice, 2 in your second, etc.*)
   - ☐ Evening ☐ Day trip ☐ Weekend ☐ Longer

3. How much would you be willing to pay for a trip?
   - ☐ Less than £5
   - ☐ £5–£10
   - ☐ £10–20
   - ☐ Over £20

4. Any other suggestions or comments?

Using the questionnaire

The sample

You cannot give the questionnaire to **all** the students, so you have to take a *representative* sample of students. Choose this sample carefully. If you only hand out the questionnaire in the common room, you will only find out the views of the sort of students who use the common room. If 40% of all the students are part-time students, then 40% of your questionnaires should go to part-time students.

Replies

Your results are affected by the number of questionnaires that are returned. If 10 out of 15 questionnaires are in favour of something, this may seem to be overwhelming support. But if the 15 questionnaires were the only replies you received from a sample of 60 questionnaires sent out, then this support only amounts to 1 person in 6. Statistics must be treated with care.

Reports

A report is a way of presenting detailed information clearly. The information is made clear by organising it into different sections. Each section is numbered and has a heading to explain what information it contains. These sections are divided into smaller subsections where necessary.

Reports are therefore very useful whenever something needs to be discussed and decided. So, a report on your market research will help your organisation to make the best decision about what trip to organise.

Producing a report

A title to indicate what the report is about.

Write in a neutral matter-of-fact style. Try to avoid putting in your own feelings or opinions, except in the Conclusion.

It is important to show clearly what is a main section and what is a subsection. Put main headings in capitals. Subheadings should be in smaller letters, set in from the margin, and have a different numbering or lettering system.

Line up the different types of headings and sections.

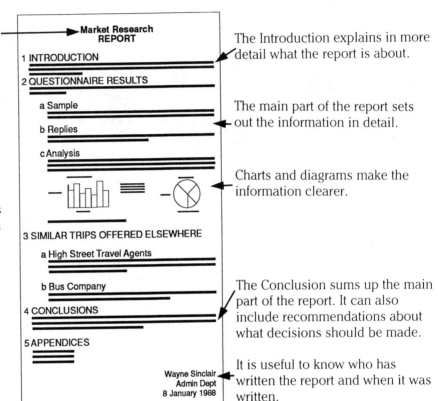

The Introduction explains in more detail what the report is about.

The main part of the report sets out the information in detail.

Charts and diagrams make the information clearer.

The Conclusion sums up the main part of the report. It can also include recommendations about what decisions should be made.

It is useful to know who has written the report and when it was written.

You have to decide on your own sections and headings when writing a report. Choose ones which make the information as clear as possible.

Numbering the headings

Instead of		You can have	
1		1	
2		2	
	a		2.1
	b		2.2
	c		2.3
3		3	
	a		3.1
	b		3.2
4		4	
5		5	

Reference books

Much of business and administrative work involves finding information from reference books, as for example in travel agency work. However, reference books can be frustrating and confusing unless you know how to go about using them.

How to use reference books

Before you can use a reference book, you have to find out what information it contains, how it is organised, and what the symbols and abbreviations mean. Look for the following features.

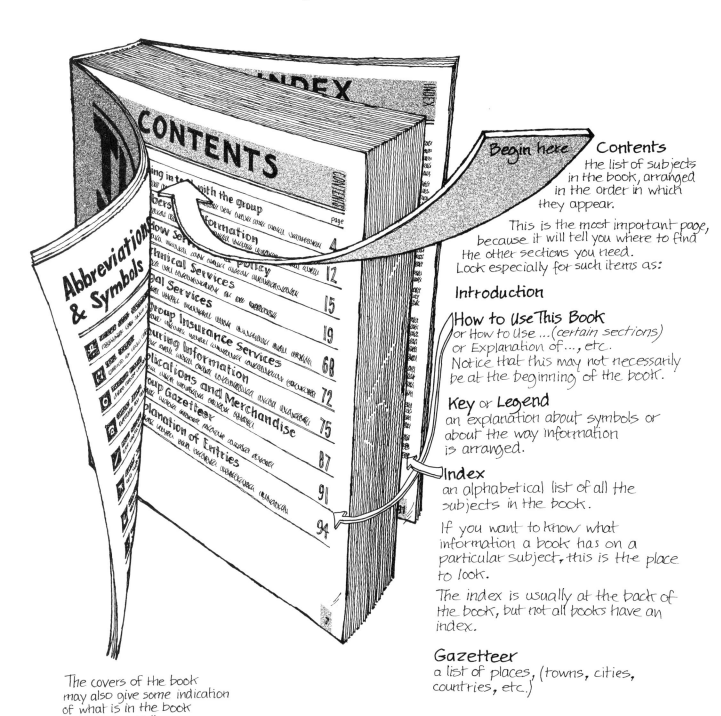

Begin here

Contents
the list of subjects in the book, arranged in the order in which they appear.

This is the most important page, because it will tell you where to find the other sections you need. Look especially for such items as:

Introduction

How to Use This Book
or How to Use...(certain sections) or Explanation of..., etc.
Notice that this may not necessarily be at the beginning of the book.

Key or Legend
an explanation about symbols or about the way information is arranged.

Index
an alphabetical list of all the subjects in the book.

If you want to know what information a book has on a particular subject, this is the place to look.

The index is usually at the back of the book, but not all books have an index.

Gazetteer
a list of places, (towns, cities, countries, etc.)

The covers of the book may also give some indication of what is in the book and how to use it.

Graphs and charts

A series of figures and statistics is not easy to understand quickly. Graphs and charts convey the information much more clearly, and also reveal trends. Your questionnaire results and your market research report will be clearer with graphs and charts.

Choosing the right sort of graph or chart

Line graphs to show how something changes. Eg, the rise and fall of the temperature in a room.

Bar charts for comparisons *and* sudden changes. Eg, numbers of men and women off work ill each day.

Pie charts to show how a *total amount* is divided up. Eg, how a certain amount of money is spent.

Pictograms for eye-catching, easy-to-understand comparisons. Eg, different-sized companies.

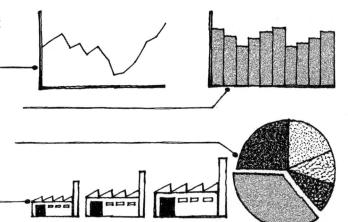

How to draw graphs and charts

Graphs and bar charts

1 Work out the highest and lowest number you will need on each scale, ie on each edge of the graph.
2 Draw the two scales. The quantity that goes up and down, eg temperature, number of men and women, should go on the vertical, the up-and-down, scale. Time usually goes on the horizontal scale.
3 Provide a title, label both scales ('£', 'Number of employees', etc.) and label each graph line, or provide a key:
♀ = women, ♂ = men, etc. for bar charts.

Pie charts

1 Find out what the total is, eg to find the total number of employees you might need to add together the male and female employees.
2 Find out how much of the total each part is, eg female employees could be a third of the workforce. You might want to express this as a percentage (see page 59).
3 Divide up the pie chart to match the size of each part, eg a third of the pie would be female employees.
4 Provide a title, and label each division of the pie, or attach a key:
▨ = female employees, etc.

How to read and interpret graphs and charts

Study the *titles*, *scales* and *labels*. These are the key to understanding what the graph is about.

To take readings from a graph, you read up from one scale until you reach the line, and then go across to the other scale.

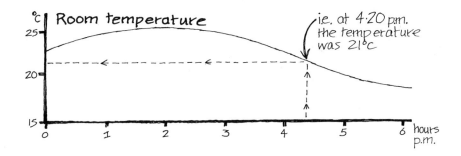

Publicity materials

No matter how good your product is, you have to publicise it in order to sell it. To see how to produce really effective publicity materials, you need to study lots of professional examples. Collect advertisements and leaflets that you find persuasive. Try to analyse what it is that makes them effective: the visual images, the associations, an appeal to vanity or fears, the use of language? Here are a few tips.

Layout and design
The overall appearance needs to be attractive and eye-catching. See Activity 2, page 40.

Headings and slogans
You need one or two main headings and also some minor ones. Try to find snappy, arresting expressions. A standard trick is to use words that begin with the same letter: Live/London, Boogie/Boat.

Wording
Make your language persuasive. Use plenty of appealing, evocative words: glamour, excitement, latest, stars, floodlit.

Publicity ideas

- Make announcements at Student Union meetings and assemblies. Negotiate a visit to each class or tutorial group to give a sales talk. Make sure that Reception is always staffed and ready with information and tickets.
- Place advertising posters and stickers on notice-boards. Hand out leaflets in the refectory or canteen.
- To sell trips to local community groups, pensioners, etc., advertise in the local library, post offices, shop windows, and the local paper. Write a press release, a short, purely factual statement sent to the newspaper, and try to get the paper interested in writing an article and taking photographs. Use your contacts, for example the Chair of the Parent-Teacher Association.

Databases

A database is a filing system on a computer. It is better than a manual system consisting of filing cabinets, etc., because the computer can sort through files when you want information. This is how it works.

In your travel agency you need to keep records of your customers. A database is like a card-index, with a different card for each customer.

In a database, the whole cardbox is called a *file*; each card is called a *record*; and each entry on the card is a *field*.

Finding information on a database

The computer finds information for you, but it does much more than simply finding a customer's card or record. It can analyse records for you in different ways. For example, it could find:
All the customers who have booked to go on a particular trip.
All the customers who live in a certain area.
All the customers who owe money.

Or it could sort the records into:
Alphabetical order of customers' names.
Date order of booking.

So if you want to send a reminder to all the customers who have not paid in full two weeks before departure, you simply instruct the computer to find this information for you and print it out. If the database is linked to word processing software, the computer can even automatically print out a reminder letter to each of these customers.

Large databases

Large organisations, such as supermarket companies, will usually have a national database on a mainframe computer.

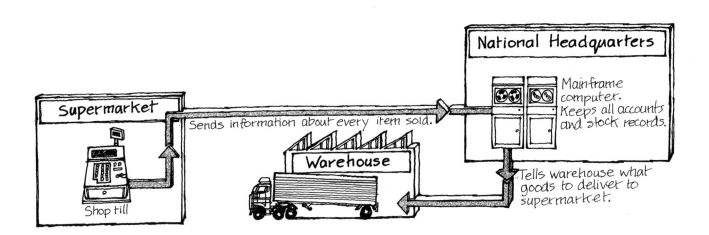

Assessment profile

This profile helps you assess what you have learnt in this activity. You should aim to have achieved at least Level 2 in every section, and Level 3 in most sections. Work with a colleague to fill in the profile, making sure you can convince your colleague that you have achieved each level. Tick each level that you have achieved.

	Level 1	**Level 2**	**Level 3**	**Level 4**
Travel agencies	Can explain in outline what a travel agency does.	Can explain in detail the work of a travel agency.	Can describe your employment and career prospects in the travel industry.	Can relate travel and tourism employment to your personal interests and abilities.
Market research	Can explain what is meant by the term market research.	Can explain why market research is necessary.	Can explain how market research is carried out.	Have successfully carried out a market research exercise.
Questionnaires	Can explain the purpose of a questionnaire.	Can describe the different types of questions which can be used in a questionnaire.	Can explain why the target group and purpose must be identified precisely.	Can explain why the sample and the number of replies must be considered.
Reports	Can explain the purpose of a report.	Can describe how a report is set out.	Can describe the main features of a report.	Have produced a business report to an acceptable standard.
Reference books	Can give three examples of reference books.	Can explain how to use a reference book: which sections to look for and why.	Can explain contents, key index, legend and gazetteer.	Have obtained information from at least five different reference books.
Graphs and charts	Can describe different types of graphs and charts.	Can describe the different uses of graphs, bar charts, pie charts and pictograms.	Can demonstrate how to draw each type of graph and chart.	Have successfully drawn each type of graph and chart and read information from them.
Publicity materials	Can describe different types of publicity materials.	Can explain what features make publicity materials effective.	Have analysed the design, headings and wording of several professional examples.	Can describe other means of publicising trips and outings.
Databases	Can explain what a database is.	Can explain why a database is better than a manual system.	Can explain the advantages of a database being connected to other software.	Can demonstrate using a database on a computer.

Date completed _____   Signed _____

Charity fund-raising

In this activity you use your organisation to raise funds for charity. This could be anything from organising a sponsored event to running a high street charity shop. You could raise funds for a well-known national charity, or for a small local charity, such as a youth club or a hospital appeal.

Understanding charities

A charity is an organisation which is set up not to make money, but to help people. Oxfam helps starving people in other countries. Shelter helps homeless people in this country. Some charities help sick people by paying for medical research, some charities protect the countryside and historic buildings and some charities help animals. Private schools and religious organisations are also allowed to be charities, although they only help their own members.

Charities are private sector institutions because they are set up by private individuals, not by the government (see page 119). They are the market economy's way of dealing with people in need. In a planned economy, the government tries to ensure that the country's wealth is shared out so that people are not in need (see page 113). Some charities therefore believe that the best way to try to help people is to put pressure on the government to take a more active role and to make changes. For example, it is argued that famine in Africa is caused mainly by the way the Western World trades with African countries. The African countries have to grow coffee for Britain instead of food for their own starving people.

> **Finding out more about charities**
>
> For information on charities in general see the September 1984 *Which?* magazine, available in most libraries. Names and telephone numbers of local and national charities can be found in *Yellow Pages*. You can then contact the local offices of those charities you are interested in to find out more information.

How to fund-raise for charities

Stage 1	*Finding out about charities* This involves finding out what charities there are, locally and nationally, thinking about which charity you would like to support, finding out what work they do, and obtaining addresses where you could contact them.
Stage 2	*Deciding what fund-raising activities you could offer* The meeting needs to consider whether to contact a charity to offer administrative assistance, such as helping in the running of a charity shop, or whether to mount a fund-raising event and donate the funds to the charity.
Stage 3	*Contacting the charity* This stage can be left out if you decide simply to raise money and then hand it over to the charity of your choice. But remember that you may want to contact the charity for help in fund-raising, perhaps for publicity leaflets or a video or a guest speaker.
Stage 4	*Planning the fund-raising* Now that you have decided which charity to support, and how you are going to raise money, the meeting needs to agree on an action plan about how the event will be organised and who will do what.
Stage 5	*Fund-raising* This may include booking rooms and equipment, obtaining whatever goods and services are needed, publicising the event, organising the procedures and staffing, and, finally, managing the event or activity itself. (See Activity 4 for more details.)
Stage 6	*Review meeting* This meeting discusses whether the fund-raising was successful, how much money was raised, and what conclusions can be drawn, especially if your organisation is to organise more fund-raising events.

Fund-raising activities

Sales events:

- *Jumble sales, bring-and-buy sales* People donate unwanted clothes and household items *in good condition*, and you sell them to raise money.
- *Car boot sales* Use the school or college car-park. People sell their unwanted goods from the boot of their cars and keep the money themselves. You raise money by charging an entrance fee to the cars and the customers.
- *Selling charity goods*, eg, Oxfam Christmas cards.
- *Summer fairs, fêtes, bazaars, etc.* A grander version of a jumble sale, usually with side-shows, stunts, catering, a celebrity and general razzmatazz.

Sponsorship events

These are events in which people agree to sponsor the participants at so much a mile or so much a minute. Such events need to be bizarre and remarkable so that they attract interest and sponsors. Avoid the usual ones, such as sponsored walks, sponsored spaghetti-eating, sponsored silences. Try to think of something new and different. You might get some ideas from looking in the *Guinness Book of Records*.

Stunts

The idea of a stunt is to do something which attracts attention and publicity. Then you charge people for admission or participation, or you simply ask for donations, using collecting boxes. An example of a stunt is laying a mile of pennies. Get police permission to use a public area such as a shopping centre, where there will be plenty of people to donate pennies. Another example is a balloon race. Each balloon carries a stamped, addressed card with the competitor's name on it offering a reward to the person returning the winning card, the one attached to the balloon which travels the furthest distance. Look in *Yellow Pages* under 'Balloons' for suppliers of the necessary equipment, or consult the *Woman's Own* book referred to below.

Events

Discos, fashion shows, etc., with the profits donated to charity. See Activity 4.

Running your own charity shop

You could operate a regular charity shop of your own in your school or college, or perhaps in high street premises. Visit a high street charity shop to see how it is done.

What each department does

	Reception	Records	Accounts	Administration
Stage 1	MEETING to decide how tasks should be divided between Departments.			
	Verbal information-gathering, eg telephone calls.	Records of charities contacted and information gathered.	Task to be decided by meeting.	Writes enquiry letters. Answers information requests made at the meeting.
Stage 2		MEETING		
	A Reception person chairs meeting.		Drafts costings and pricings for meeting.	Takes minutes of meeting.
Stage 3	Contacts charity in person and by telephone. Typing.	Keeps records of all contacts and arrangements made.	Provides draft costings and pricings for events discussed with charity.	Contacts charity in writing and/or sends letters of confirmation.
Stage 4	MEETING to decide how tasks should be divided between departments.			
	A Reception person chairs meeting.		Detailed costings and pricings for meeting.	Takes minutes of meeting.
Stage 5	Makes arrangements by telephone and in person. Sales, typing and reception duties.	Co-ordinates action plan and arrangements made by each Department. Stock control.	Handles purchases, book-keeping, bank account and cash.	Writes letters. Publicity materials. Signs and notices.
Stage 6		MEETING		
	A Reception person chairs meeting.		Presents Receipts and Payments Account.	Takes minutes of meeting.

Other tips

Combine ideas

Put different fund-raising ideas together. Combine a jumble sale with a sponsored event and some stunts. Or hold a special collecting day. For example, an Oxfam Day in your school or college could have Oxfam publicity posters and films, class projects on Oxfam, stunts and sponsored events, collections, and a special presentation ceremony when the Chair of the Governors or a local celebrity hands over the money raised to an official of the charity.

Publicity

You need the maximum publicity to get as many donations as possible. Use plenty of publicity materials provided both by yourselves and by the charity concerned. Try to interest the local newspapers or radio station in covering your fund-raising. Send them a *press release*, a short factual statement in double-spaced typing. If your fund-raising is particularly interesting or unusual, the newspaper might send a photographer to cover the event.

Commercial sponsorship

Try to get the support of local businesses. They may be interested not only for the sake of helping a charity, but also to obtain some publicity for their own goods and services. For example, a local fashion shop or department store might be willing to lend clothes for a fashion show, or a hamburger restaurant might provide the hamburgers for a sponsored hamburger-eating event.

Administrative help to charities

Your organisation might also be able to support charities by offering administrative help in the charity's local offices or shop.

For other ideas and useful advice on fund-raising, see the *Woman's Own Book of Fund-Raising* (William Collins and Sons, 1986).

Spreadsheets

Spreadsheet software allows you to perform calculations on large amounts of information. Spreadsheets are especially good when calculations have to be repeated a number of times.

Figures in brackets [ ] can be calculated from other figures:
Total = January + February
Value of Sales = Selling Price × Quantity sold
Profit = Value of Sales − Total Costs

What happens if material costs rise to £25?
What happens if the sales department revises the figures for quantities to 54 and 63?

On a spreadsheet calculator these questions would be easy to answer. You simply type in the new figures for sales and the program calculates the new profit figures. Spreadsheets will let you add new rows and columns as well. So you could add forecasts for March and April with ease.

```
Profit forecast for ABC Amplifiers Ltd

Selling price = £100     Materials cost = £20

                    Jan        Feb        Total

Quantity sold        50         65        [  115]
Value of sales    [5700]     [6500]       [11500]

Costs:
  labour          2000       2000         [4000]
  materials       [1000]     [1300]       [2300]
  rent            150         150         [ 300]
  rates           100         100         [ 200]
  other           400         400         [ 800]
Total costs       [3650]     [3950]       [7600]
PROFIT            [1350]     [2550]       [3900]
```

A typical spreadsheet work screen

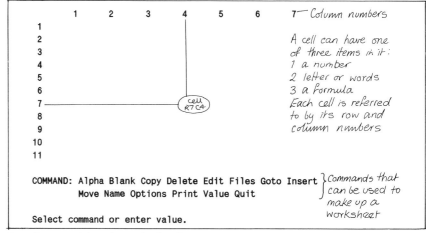

Use of a spreadsheet by a charity shop

7 — Column numbers

A cell can have one of three items in it:
1 a number
2 letter or words
3 a formula
Each cell is referred to by its row and column numbers

Commands that can be used to make up a worksheet

Headings entered using the Alpha command
Words in column 1 are also entered using the Alpha command

Some useful commands
Insert command can be used to create a new column for March if it is needed
Goto command can be used to pick out any cell
Move command is used to move rows or columns
Copy is used to copy rows or columns

These cells will have formulae to calculate the totals. Entered using the value command

90

Student advice and information centre

In this activity you set up and run a service to provide information that is useful to students while they are at college, or on work experience, or looking for a job.

This gives you more practice in business and administration, since gathering and organising information is a typical business activity. In addition, you learn about various topics which are important for you at school or college and at work: employment and consumer rights, health and safety at work, trade unions, the internal structure of organisations, and the role of central and local government.

How to operate an information centre

Stage 1	*A Meeting* to decide on which topics to provide information. The meeting needs to draw up a detailed action plan showing which Departments will gather what information by when. Further meetings may be needed at later stages of this activity.
Stage 2	*Obtaining information* on each topic. The allocation of this task between Departments will depend on the topics chosen and the type of information required.
Stage 3	*Producing the leaflets*, fact sheets, etc. The Administration Department may need help from the other three Departments, since the main task is the designing and writing of the leaflets.
Stage 4	*Meeting* to decide on how to operate the service: dates, times and arrangements for personal interviews to give advice on specific topics.
Stage 5	*Running the service* This means advertising the Centre and staffing it, dealing with enquiries, and providing personal information and advice on specific topics. People from each Department should be available to offer information on topics they have researched. The centre's information can also be put into a viewdata system (see page 103).

What information to provide

These are the main areas in which you can provide information. To find out about these areas you will need to follow the suggestions set out in the pages of this activity. You will also need to consult the Reference pages at the end of the book.

Employment and work experience

What to look for in a job: why some job opportunities are better than others.
Employment rights: what legal rights you have and how to defend them.
Trade unions including the Students Union in your school or college: what they are, how they operate, what benefits they offer, and whether people should join one when they start work.
Health and Safety at Work: what dangers students and employees should be aware of, what their legal rights are, and what to do about hazards at work.

Organisational structure: understanding the organisation: what the different departments are, and what they do.
Unfair discrimination: how Equal Opportunities policies can help.

(See pages 98–9 in this Activity and Reference page 122.)

The local community

The Local Council: what it is, what services it provides, and how to find the various departments.
Local leisure facilities: a guide to local shops, discotheques, sports centres, etc.
Local help and advisory agencies: what agencies there are, what they do and who provides them.

(See page 102 in this Activity and Reference page 117.)

What each department does

	Reception	**Records**	**Accounts**	**Administration**
Stage 1	MEETING			
	A Reception person chairs meeting.			Takes minutes of meeting.
Stage 2	Each Department gathers information on a separate topic. Alternatively information-gathering tasks can be distributed amongst different departments according to departmental expertise, eg:			
	Verbal information-gathering: telephone calls and talking to people in person. Keeps written records of all discussions. Typing.	Keeps a record of names and addresses contacted and of action plan progress. Collects and combines the information gathered by other departments, eg questionnaire.	Obtains financial information: costs, prices and statistics. Analyses questionnaire results.	Writes up and circulates minutes of meeting. Writes letters and questionnaires to obtain information and leaflets. (See page 80.)
Stage 3	Types text for leaflets.	Stores and stock control of leaflets.	Produces graphs, charts and numerical information required for leaflets.	Designs leaflets and writes text.
Stage 4	MEETING			
	A Reception person chairs meeting.			Takes minutes of meeting.
Stage 5	Sets up interview areas, deals with enquiries, arranges appointments for individual advice.	Leaflet stock control, records of publicity campaign: posters, leaflets, verbal announcements, etc.	Conducts user-survey of Centre (questionnaires to each visitor to find out how many people are using Centre for which topics).	Produces publicity materials. Writes user-survey report based on Accounts' findings.

College or school information

The Students Union: what it is and what it does.
Structure and organisation of college.
Health and Safety: what students need to be aware of, what their legal rights are, and how hazards and accidents should be dealt with.
Equal Opportunities: how women and racial minorities are discriminated against in education and what can be done about it.
The College and the Local Authority: what the connections are between the two, how to apply for grants, bus passes, etc.
College Clubs, Societies and Facilities.

(See pages 96–99 in this Activity and Reference pages 122–3.)

Consumer issues

Consumer rights: what rights people have when they go shopping and when they are entitled to a refund.
Product information: how to find out which are best buys and best value for money.
Buying guides: testing products often bought by students and recommending best buys.
Guide to local shops: advice on which are the best shops and why, which shops offer students discounts, and which allow customers to exchange purchases.

(See pages 100–101 in this Activity and Reference page 124.)

Finding out more

To find out more about how information services operate visit a local Citizens' Advice Bureau. Your school or college library is also an information service; the Librarian may be able to show you how information is collected, organised and presented.

Employment

Pay and conditions, rights, trade unions

When you start to look for a job it is important to understand the realities of the world of work. In the *Standard of Living Game* you tried to obtain good deals in your buying and selling. Employment is just the same: you are entering a competitive market. What you are selling is your work, your labour. Employers will try to buy your labour as cheaply as possible; you must try to get the best deal you can. Market forces mean that people with skills or qualifications in short supply get good wages and conditions. However, wage levels are also greatly affected by attitudes, values and beliefs about how much people should be paid for different jobs. (See pages 114–5 — *The Income Parade*.)

Pay, conditions and prospects

In looking for employment you need to consider not just the wages but also:

- The hours of work and the number of holidays.
- The working conditions. Is it a comfortable, safe and attractive environment?
- Training opportunities. Does the employer provide training for a recognised qualification, or provide *day release* allowing you to attend college one day a week while being paid?
- Promotion opportunities.
- Fringe benefits: paid holidays, staff canteen, luncheon vouchers, staff discounts, etc.

Finding out about employment

To find out what happens in the real world of employment take a look at your own school or college. Find out what employment means to the different types of employees, by obtaining the information shown below. Be tactful in approaching staff. Most staff will probably be willing to discuss some aspects of their work, but for information such as pay and qualifications it may be better to speak to a union official and ask for general information, eg pay scales and job descriptions, rather than asking for details from any particular person.

What to look for in a job

You can carry out a similar survey of pay, conditions, and prospects of jobs in business and administration. Simply look at a variety of job advertisements in the local press, and try to obtain the information shown in the chart below. This should give you a reasonable idea of the difference between a good job opportunity and a poor one.

Legal rights

Some of the objectives unions have struggled for have now been made law. These rights give you some protection against unfair discrimination and unfair dismissal, and entitle you to a contract of employment and a safe working environment, amongst other things. However, they do not give you as much protection as union membership. It is very important that you know what your rights are. See Reference Section pages 122–3, for further information.

Survey of jobs — pay & conditions

Job	Pay	Qualifications or experience needed	Hours of work	Holidays (number of days per year)	Working conditions	Fringe benefits
Try to include all the different types of jobs eg cleaner, teacher, technician.					Clean? Warm? Normal office hours? Satisfying work? Training and promotion prospects? Personal control or constant supervision?	Canteen? Luncheon vouchers? Crèche?, etc.

Trade unions

Like buyers and sellers in any market, employers and employees have opposite aims and interests.

The **employer** wants to produce as much as possible as cheaply as possible:
- Low wages.
- High production: long hours of hard work.
- A co-operative workforce which can be controlled to suit the employer's needs. The employer wants to be able to hire and fire staff, to move staff from one task to another, and to decide how and where work will be done.

The **employee** wants job satisfaction:
- High wages.
- Interesting satisfying work.
- A pleasant and safe working environment.
- Some involvement in decision-making and some control over their working life.

But the employer has **the power** ...

The employer has the power to hire and fire, to control the work, to pay wages, etc. The employer is the boss; there is no democracy in employment. If an employee is dissatisfied and complains, the employer can ignore them or even fire them.

However ...

If all the employees act *together* then they do have some power; the employer cannot very easily sack all of them. Acting as a union gives the employees some bargaining power because they can refuse to co-operate or even go on strike. Trade unions are democratic; decisions are made through elections and voting.

So, trade unions enable employees to get better pay and conditions and to have some influence over their working lives.

Analysing your survey results

Analyse your results by using charts and graphs. Then try to answer the questions below.

- Do unionised jobs (where most employees are union members) tend to have better pay and conditions than non-unionised jobs?
- Why are some jobs much better paid than others?
- Why are people who do dirty unpleasant jobs paid less than those who do clean comfortable jobs? Is this fair? Is it necessary?
- Should the difference between the lowest paid and highest paid be as great as it is? Should it be bigger? (See also pages 114–5.)

and Trade union benefits			
Trade union name	**Size of membership** (% of employees)	**Main union activities**	**Main benefits of union membership**
Don't forget to include the National Union of Students.	Eg, 70% of teachers in the school are union members.	Ask union officials. Pay negotiations? Disputes? Safety?	How are employees better off because of the union.

Health and safety at work

Every year thousands of people are killed or seriously injured at work. It is very important to be aware of health and safety at work. The best way to familiarise yourself with this is to investigate health and safety in your own school or college, as described in Sections 1 to 4 below. The Reference section (page 123) gives you the basic information you need about the law and procedures.

1 How safe is your school or college?

Make yourself a checklist covering the areas shown in this diagram and use it to inspect your school or college building.

Building and tidiness

1 Is the floor slippery?
2 Are there handrails on stairways?
  Is there enough space in all classrooms and workshops?
3 Are waste-bins provided?
4 Are work areas tidy?

Environment

5 Is lighting adequate?
6 Is the building ventilated?
7 Is the temperature comfortable?
8 Is different lighting provided for VDU work?

2 Equipment

The equipment you see may need handling with care. Copy and fill in the chart below, listing all the equipment used on your course.

Machine Equipment	Possible Dangers	Precautions to be taken
VDU Screen Automatic Stapler Guillotine	Eyestrain Injuries to fingers	Use for short periods only Use safety guard

96

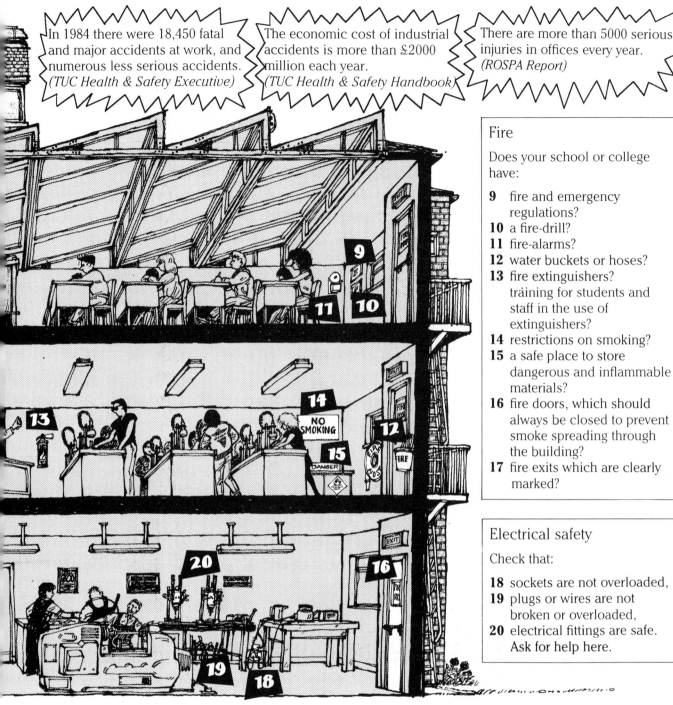

3 Health and Safety Representatives

Find out from your tutor who the staff Health and Safety Representatives are. Ask what their duties are. They may tell you how Health and Safety inspections are carried out. They may be interested to see the results of your inspection.

4 Accidents

Check who the first-aiders are. Find out where first-aid boxes are kept. Ask for a copy of the school or college accident form, and enquire where the accident book is kept.

You can obtain more information about health and safety by writing for information leaflets to the following organisations:

British Safety Council
National Safety Centre
Chancellor's Road
London W6 9RS

The local offices of
The Health & Safety Executive

Her Majesty's Stationery Office
49 High Holborn
London WC1V 6HB

Equal opportunities

Equal opportunities policies are attempts to stop people being treated unfairly simply because they happen to be women, or come from a different ethnic group, or have different sexual preferences, or are married or not married, or have some disability. It is not sufficient to make this sort of unfair discrimination illegal, because the real problem is people's attitudes and expectations. Very often, people unfairly discriminate against others without ever meaning to or realising that they have. Equal opportunities policies therefore concentrate on *stereotypes*, the things that form our attitudes and expectations, and *monitoring*, checking to see if people are being discriminated against. You can find out more by investigating stereotypes and by carrying out some monitoring exercises.

Stereotypes

A stereotype is a standard image. For example, women are often stereotyped as merely pretty objects or as housewives, secretaries, or nurses. They are seen as emotional, illogical, timid and in need of protection from men. In contrast, men are stereotyped as people with careers: managers and doctors. They are seen as logical, bold, aggressive, and protective to women. So, it is not surprising that girls and boys grow up to match the stereotypes they see all around them; girls therefore do not have equal opportunities with boys in careers.

Sometimes, the stereotype is simply to pretend certain people do not even exist. How often do you see a black person in advertisements? In the English language an unknown person is always 'he' (so in this book an unknown person is deliberately referred to as 'they', as in spoken English. For example: 'There's some*one* waiting outside to see you.' 'Well, tell *them* to come in.'

To investigate stereotypes, carry out a survey of the stereotypes you see around you, in school or college, on television, in people's conversation, in newspapers, films and books. Try to find as many examples as possible of damaging or insulting stereotypes which restrict people's opportunities.

Monitoring

Equal Opportunities monitoring is complex, but basically it is a matter of comparing numbers. For example, if 10% of job applicants are people of Afro-Caribbean origin, then one would expect that 10% of the work-force would be of Afro-Caribbean origin. If there are substantially less than 10% employed, it is likely that such people are being denied equal opportunities, perhaps because the selection procedures are biased against certain people.

Try some Equal Opportunities monitoring for yourself by analysing the position of say, women, in your own school or college. Although you must be careful about interpreting the results, even a crude survey is likely to reveal remarkable patterns and provoke some important questions. For example, in the survey below, it is possible that fewer women applied for more senior positions, or that women applicants were often less well qualified. On the other hand, it could be that men in senior positions tend to appoint men rather than women.

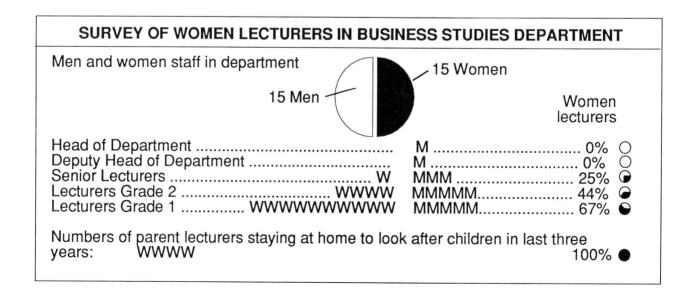

Stereotypes survey

Stereotypes of, *eg women*, as found in:

1 *Business Studies textbooks*
Eg, try counting the number of times women appear in illustrations; then count the number of times they appear as secretaries and the number of times as managers. Then do the same with illustrations of men.

2 *Advertisements*

3 *Language*
Eg, 'male' words like 'chairman', 'masterpiece', 'mankind', 'God the Father', and put-down words like 'usherette', 'slag', 'manageress', 'authoress'. In these words the -ess ending suggests the woman is not a real manager or author.

4 *Jokes*
Many jokes depend on stereotypes, for example, Irish jokes.

Question
How do you make an Irishman burn his ear?
Answer
Phone him up when he's doing the ironing.

5 *TV, films, magazines and newspapers.*

6 *Other sources*
Eg, birthday cards.

Consumer issues

When you spend your money you are being a consumer, that is, someone who consumes the goods and services provided by the economy. You need to know which products offer the best value for money and what your legal rights are. These pages suggests some ways of finding out about these issues, and the Reference Section (page 124) contains the basic background information you will need.

Product information: getting the best value for money

In theory, a market economy such as Britain's gives the consumer the best products at the best prices because the customer is able to choose freely between the different products on the market. But, in practice, the consumer may not be able to do this because of:

Lack of knowledge This applies to products which are very technical and which you do not buy regularly, for example, digital watches, video recorders, solicitors' services. So, use independent advice services, eg consumer magazines such as *Which?* magazine, and Citizens Advice Bureaux.

Advertising Advertising is now an extremely sophisticated way of influencing people. But very often it does not influence them by giving them information, but by subtle psychological methods, which make people want a product because of its image and associations, for example, television commercials for drinks and washing powders. So, be aware of how advertising manipulates you.

Monopoly means there is only one producer, so there is no choice for the consumer, for example, gas supplies (private sector), trains (public sector). The price and the quality of the product is completely in the hands of the producer. This is a major difficulty in the private sector, and still more so for the public sector. So, if you are dissatisfied, complain persistently and use the various watchdog organisations which exist to protect consumers, eg the Post Office Users' National Council.

Consumer rights

You have various legal rights to return or change unsatisfactory products, and some shops may offer additional facilities.

For further information see page 124.

Finding out about product information

1 *Buying guides* Study the product reports in *Which?* magazine. Then produce a similar guide for a type of product commonly bought by students, eg correcting fluid, pens or bubble gum.

Report on CORRECTING FLUIDS				
Name of Produce	Cost	Drying Time	Covering Power	Need for Thinner
Cover-Rite Tipe-ex Pittik				
We recommend the following products: 1 Cover-Rite because........ 2 Pittik because............ BEST BUY............				

2 *Advertising* Collect examples of advertisements, either gathered at random or relating to particular products. Analyse how they persuade: whether they provide factual information, create attractive associations, or operate on people's fears. Show, by charts and graphs, what proportion of advertisements inform the consumer, and how many simply manipulate.

This advertisement for women's perfume suggests a woman who is merely a sexy, passive object.

This advertisement for men's perfume suggests an active man, jetting off around the world.

3 *Consumer organisations* Compile a list of organisations which help dissatisfied consumers and provide consumer advice and information. Explain the services each organisation can give.

Finding out about consumer rights

Conduct a survey of local shops to find out their policies on returned goods. See if they are meeting their legal obligations and what additional rights they may offer, including student discounts.

```
QUESTIONNAIRE ON CONSUMER POLICY

1    Do you give discounts to students?     YES/NO
     If so how much? _ _ _ _ _
2    Does the shop allow customers to return goods if:
     (tick where appropriate):

          a. They are faulty?
          b. They do not work?
          c. They are not as
             described on the packet?
          d. The are not fit for the
             purpose sold?
          e. The customer decides they
             would prefer a different
             colour or shape?
          f. The customer decides they
             bought the wrong size?

3    When goods are returned, do you offer:

          a. A cash refund?
          b. To exchange the goods?
          c. A credit note?
          d. To refund the money?
```

Local community organisations

Few people are aware of all the facilities available to them in their local community, and many people have only a hazy understanding of what organisations provide which services and how those organisations are structured. You can produce information leaflets which explain these matters, and provide useful details of telephone numbers, locations and opening hours.

Finding out about the local community and organisations

- The Reference Section will give you the basic background information you will need.
- The *Thomson Local Directory* Community Pages are a very useful source of information, and may also give you some ideas about how to present the information.
- Detailed information will be available from libraries and the Information Department of the local authority.

Here are some local community topics on which you could produce information leaflets. You may also be able to think up additional topics.

Help and advisory agencies

Eg, Citizens Advice bureaux, the Samaritans, agencies which help with drug addiction, the Careers Service, RSPCA, Trading Standards Office.

Include in your leaflet:
  the name of the organisation,
  what it does,
  who provides the service: central or local government, charity, commercial organisation?
  details of services offered,
  address, telephone number, opening hours.

Local council
Produce a short guide to the local council.
Explain:
- what it is,
- how it is related to central government,
- what services it provides,
- where to find the different Departments,
- how to apply for grants, bus passes, etc.

School or college guide

Explain the structure of the organisation and its relationship to the local council. Give details of services and facilities offered, such as counselling, careers information, sports, clubs and societies, health and safety matters.

Leisure
Sport and recreation facilities

Give details of:

- sports centres, swimming-pools, tennis courts etc, including your school or college facilities,
- local clubs and societies,
- discotheques,
- theatres and cinemas,
- museums, galleries, exhibitions,
- shops and markets, especially those relevant to students (bookshops, stationers, fashion shops, music shops, etc.).

Explain which organisations provide these services, what student discounts may be offered, and mention any events or exhibitions which might be of particular interest to students. Also include addresses, telephone numbers, opening hours, etc.

Structure of organisations

Provide information which would be useful to students when they are on work experience placements or entering employment. Include the different types of organisations in the economy and how they are structured internally. If possible, describe the structure of an actual local company or organisation.

Local information

Compile a checklist of names, addresses, telephone numbers and opening hours of local organisations and services which people need from time to time.

Viewdata

A viewdata system is a way of providing information on computers. Instead of looking in reference books, timetables and newspapers, you simply call up pages of information on your computer screen. This is better than printed information because it always gives the very latest up-to-the-minute information. Better still, you can communicate with the system to make bookings or purchases.

You can often see a viewdata system being used in travel agents. It might be used, for example, to find a suitable flight for a customer. The travel agent would then book seats on the flight using the viewdata terminal.

Britain has a national viewdata system available to the public called *Prestel*. Teletext services, *Ceefax* (BBC) and *Oracle* (ITV), are similar; they broadcast pages of information to television sets, but you cannot communicate with them.

Setting up a viewdata system

Viewdata software allows you to create your own viewdata system. To create pages you need a page, or *frame*, editor. To put the pages in the correct place in the system you need a *tree editor*.

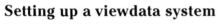

Viewdata tree of pages.
The frames 4a, 4b, 4c make up page 4.

Steps

Decide what information to put on the system.
Decide how pages will be connected.
Create and insert pages.

Using viewdata in an information centre

Decide the subjects on which advice is to be given, for example, the local community, college information, health and safety, trade unions, consumer rights. Make up a tree for the system and make sure it is easy to get to pages of information by having menu pages. Design menus and information pages and put them in the tree.

Menu pages

By following the menu pages you will get to information pages that tell you what you want to know. If you already know which page the information is on, you can jump straight to that page. The tree editor lets you link keys to pages. When you are looking at page 0, pressing key 1 takes you to page 8 so you do not have to match page numbers.

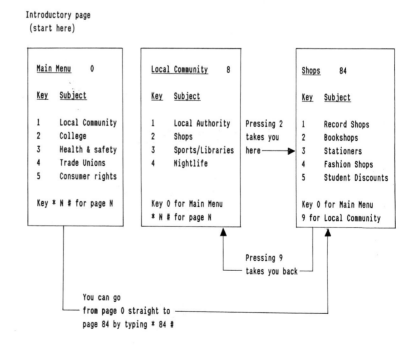

Assessment profile

This profile helps you assess what you have learnt in this activity. You should aim to have achieved at least Level 2 in every section, and Level 3 in most sections. Work with a colleague to fill in the profile, making sure you can convince your colleague that you have achieved each level. Tick each level that you have achieved.

	Level 1	Level 2	Level 3	Level 4
Employment rights, pay & conditions	Can explain what 'rights', 'pay and conditions' mean.	Can give examples of differences in pay and conditions of various jobs.	Can explain rights relating to job recruitment, dismissal and Health and Safety.	Can give some explanation of differences in pay and conditions, and how to defend rights.
Trade unions	Can explain what a trade union is.	Can explain why trade unions are necessary.	Can give examples of main benefits to trade union membership.	Have investigated the role of trade unions in education and office jobs.
Health and Safety at work	Can explain why Health and Safety at work is important.	Can describe the main dangers in school or college and in the office.	Can describe the main features of Health and Safety laws.	Can describe procedures to be followed for hazards and accidents.
Equal opportunities	Can give examples of unequal opportunities and racial or sexual discrimination.	Can explain why stereotypes and monitoring are important.	Can explain what protection is provided by the law and by trade unions.	Can explain how Equal Opportunities policies operate.
Consumer rights	Can explain what is meant by 'consumer rights'.	Can explain in detail the customer's legal rights.	Can describe how to obtain product information.	Can explain how advertising and monopolies restrict consumers.
Organisational structure	Can explain what is meant by the 'structure' of an organisation.	Can explain how your school or college is structured.	Can describe the structure of a large company or local authority.	Have studied the structure of an actual organisation.
Central and local Government	Can explain in outline what central and local government do.	Can explain the difference between Parliament, government and the civil service.	Can describe the structure of a local authority.	Can explain and comment on views and beliefs of different political parties.
Viewdata	Can explain what a viewdata system is.	Can give examples of viewdata systems.	Can explain how a viewdata system operates.	Have seen or operated a viewdata system.

Date completed _____   Signed _____

Student publication

In this activity you use your organisation to publish a newspaper or magazine to sell in your school or college. The main task for your organisation is not to write the articles, but to deal with the business and administrative aspects of producing a publication. These include market research, arranging for people to write the articles, selling advertising space, 'printing' the required number of copies and selling them.

WRITE TO REPLY

Inside this term's bumper edition

	Page
Features	2
Sports	4
Your problems	6
Crossword	7
Jobsearch	9
Quiz	10
Gossip	12
Fashion	13
Review	14

STUDENT TIMES

Issue No. 1   20p

The No. 1 Student Newspaper!

SHOCK HORROR! CANTEEN PRICES TO RISE BY 25%

Students and staff will be shocked to hear that the local Education Authority has decided to withdraw all subsidies from school and college canteens. This could mean a rise of up to 25% on some of the prices in our own canteen.

THE £1 SAUSAGE

A plate of sausage, chips and beans could cost you over a pound! Can students, already struggling to survive on inadequate grants, tolerate this latest attack on their living standards?

UNION ACTION

Darren Bailey Students Union President, is organising a petition which he hopes to present to the Authority's Education Sub-committee at its next meeting. Darren is calling on all staff and students to sign this petition. The next stage in the campaign against the Authority's decision could be a boycott of the canteen.

NO COMMENT

Ms Biggs, canteen Manager, when questioned by our intrepid reporter, Alice Hope, only said, 'No comment.'
(Continued on back page)

Mr John Ogilvey, known to most students as Old Ogle has announced his engagement to Ms Cynthia Hunt, a bank clerk, who was a student at this college three years ago. Mr Ogilvey has taught in the Department of Business Studies for the past twenty three years.

We asked Mr Ogilvey if his forthcoming marriage to Ms Hunt was likely to make any difference to
(continued on p.3)

ADVERTISEMENT

SPORTICUS

For all your sportswear and equipment

27 High Street, Westbury.

Although your main task is not to write the newspaper or magazine you will need to edit it. Editing is supervising the content of the publication, that is deciding what articles and features there should be, making any necessary alterations to the articles after they have been written, and designing the layout of the pages, including the headlines. You will therefore need an Editorial Department. Of course, you might also enjoy writing some of the articles and features yourselves.

How to publish a newspaper or magazine

In this activity you need an Editorial Department. This could simply be a fifth department, but it may be better to combine the Accounts and Records departments. Reception is responsible for the reprographics, that is printing the required number of copies.

Stage 1	*Considering what type of magazine or newspaper you could publish* A serious publication? A jokey one? A mixture of both? Will it concentrate on news, and, if so, just college news, or outside events too? Will it be a magazine concentrating on feature articles? Will the features be on music, fashion, student life-styles, politics, student issues, science fiction, humour, sport? What sort of name and image will it have?
Stage 2	*Market research* Finding out the kinds of publication, articles and features which will interest your potential customers and how much they would be willing to pay for the publication.
Stage 3	*Deciding on the type of publication*: its name and image, planning the contents. *Costing and pricing*: cost of materials and reprographics; likely sales; selling price and advertising rates based on market research and total student numbers. *Inviting students and staff to submit articles*, features, photographs, etc.
Stage 4	*Selling advertising space and commissioning articles* Persuade local shopkeepers, businesses and organisations to place advertisements in your publication. Decide which articles, features, photographs, etc, to commission. Agree details and deadlines in writing with writers, photographers, cartoonists, etc.

Ideas for articles and features

Interviews with local celebrities.
What people think of the college.
What it's like to be an overseas student in this country.
Information on student grants, finding accommodation, part-time jobs, etc.

Letters to the Editor.
Problem page.
Horoscope.
Cartoons.

Jokes.
Short stories.
Puzzles and crosswords.
What's on locally: discos, films, clubs, sports, etc.

Commissioning articles

To find people who would be willing to contribute articles, photographs, cartoons, etc. you can:

Advertise for contributors.

Ask teachers if they would make contributions part of their classwork.

- English and Communications teachers could set assignments in writing articles, short stories and crossword puzzles.
- Literature and Film Studies teachers could set assignments in writing reviews of current plays, films and television programmes.
- Photography teachers could set assignments in taking photographs for the publication.
- Art teachers could set assignments on cartoons and illustrations.

Approach particular people

- Students' Union President for an article on the Students Union.
- Staff for an article or interview on *A day in the life of a caretaker/secretary/teacher/cleaner, etc.*
- Clubs and societies. For example, the Chess Club could contribute a chess puzzle.

When you have found people willing to be contributors, discuss their contribution with them in detail. Agree the content, the length and the deadline. Then confirm these details in writing, and keep in regular contact with them to make sure they keep to the deadline.

What each department does

	Editorial	**Reception and Reprographics**	**Accounts and Records**	**Administration**
Stage 1	Editorial staff presents ideas to meeting.	M E E T I N G A Reception person chairs meeting.		Takes minutes of meeting.
Stage 2	Sketches out different possible types of publication for questionnaire.	Types and distributes questionnaire. Types Market Research Report.	Analyses questionnaire results (% in favour, bar charts, etc.).	Devises questionnaire and writes Market Research Report.
Stage 3	Decides name and image. Plans contents (articles, photos etc.). Designs layout.	M E E T I N G Chairs meeting. Types and reproduces publicity inviting contributions.	Explains analysis of questionnaire results. Action plan progress. Costing and pricing.	Explains Report's recommendations. Takes minutes. Publicity inviting contributions.
Stage 4	Decides which articles, etc. to commission.	Types letters/memos confirming commissions. Sells advertising space.	Opens accounts. Handles advertising money.	Writes confirmations of commissioned articles and deadlines.

Turn the next page for Stages 5 to 7.

Selling advertising space

Contact your local newspaper. Find out how much they charge people who want to place advertisements in their newspaper. What proportion of the newspaper's income comes from advertising? What proportion comes from newspaper sales?

Write to local shopkeepers and organisations, or visit them in person. Tell them about your publication and ask them to advertise their goods or services in your publication.

When you contact local shopkeepers and organisations, you will need to tell them:

The name of your school or college.

That you are producing a magazine as part of your course.

That you hope to raise enough money to cover the magazine's production costs by selling advertising space.

That you would like them to advertise their goods or services in the magazine.

That you are prepared either to design the advertisement yourselves or to copy any material that the shopkeepers already have.

How much you charge for advertising in the magazine. Remember to quote different prices for advertisements of different sizes.

Stage 5	*Editing and typing the newspaper or magazine* Edit articles and features to be included in your publication, type and proof-read them. Paste up pages for photocopying (see page 42). *Progress chase* ie, regularly contact contributors to keep them to deadlines.
Stage 6	*Printing and publicising the newspaper or magazine* Use office reprographics machinery to produce the required number of copies (see page 110). Advertise the publication.
Stage 7	*Selling the newspaper or magazine to students and staff* Distribute copies to sales points throughout the college. Handle cash and keep accounts.

These are the stages needed for each publication. You can produce several different publications at the same time. You might also want to consider other types of publication, such as regular bulletins and information sheets for Departments or committees within the college, or for clubs and societies.

Tips on editing

Make sure your cover or front page is eye-catching and attractive.

Use plenty of photographs and illustrations. Pictures with captions can be more interesting than words by themselves.

When editing articles, make any alterations you think will improve them. For example:

- Try to get the main point of the article in the first sentence, and certainly in the first paragraph. This attracts the reader's attention. Later paragraphs should go into greater detail.
- Give articles bold dramatic headlines.
- Add a final paragraph that sums up what the writer has said and leads to some firm conclusion.
- Cut out any uninteresting or irrelevant paragraphs.
- Ask the writer for more details or examples if the article is too vague.
- Correct any mistakes you find in the spelling, punctuation or wording of the article.

MR ~~OGILVEY~~ LECTURER TO WED

~~Most readers know~~ Mr ~~John~~ Ogilvey, ~~who~~ has taught in the Department of Business Studies for the past twenty-three years.

Mr Ogilvey, know to most students as Old Ogle has announced his engagement to Ms Cynthia Hunt, a bank clerk who was a student at this college three years ago.

~~Mr~~ Ogilvey was until recently the ~~constant~~ companion of a certain ~~member of the~~ office staff who will remain nameless.

We asked Mr Ogilvey if his forthcoming marriage to Ms Hunt is likely to make any difference to

What each department does

	Editorial	Reception and Reprographics	Accounts and Records	Administration
Stage 5	Edits articles and features. Pastes up pages.	Types and proof-reads articles. Pastes up pages.	Stock control of materials and pasted-up pages. Keeps accounts.	Progress-chases contributors.
Stage 6	Produces publicity materials to advertise publication.	Prints required number of copies on reprographic machinery.	Stock control of printed copies. Publicity records. Keeps accounts.	Produces publicity materials. Prepares sales arrangements.
Stage 7	Distributes and sells publication.	Distributes and sells publication.	Stock control. Cash and accounts.	Controls sales arrangements.

The layout of your publication

Collect examples of newspapers and magazines. Study their layouts and presentation, and decide which ones you find attractive and why. This will help you to design the layout of your publication. You will need to consider:

- The amount of space to be used for photographs, drawings and other illustrations.
- How much space to give to articles, and how much to advertisements.
- Whether the articles are to be typed in columns, or straight across the page. You will find a word processor makes typing and layout considerably easier.
- The size of your headlines and titles.

> Finding out more
>
> You can find out more by visiting a publisher or a newspaper office.
>
> Enquire about editing, the administrative work involved in publishing, and about selling advertising space.

Reprographics

Reprographics means producing multiple copies of documents (*repro*ducing the original document many times). These are the main machines used for reprographics. See which of these are available to you for producing copies of your magazine or newspaper.

Photocopiers

These are the best machines for office reprographics, but the copies are expensive.

To produce good photocopies

- Your original document must be clean and sharp, with dark typing and drawings. Use a new ribbon in your typewriter or printer, and use an ink drawing pen for any diagrams.

- Make sure the glass plate is clean. Any dust or greasy marks will appear on the photocopy.
- Study the manual and make full use of the photocopier's controls.
- Don't use ordinary correcting fluid to alter or clean up photocopied documents before photocopying them again. Use the specially designed photocopier correcting fluids, which will not smear.

You can include photographs in your documents, but only black and white photographs with a strong contrast between black and white will photocopy well. See page 40–41 for details of paste-up technique.

A photocopier

Duplicating machines

These are a cheaper, messier way of producing multiple copies, and the quality is much poorer.

Spirit duplicators are the cheapest. You have to type, write or draw the original document on a special piece of paper. You can only run off a few dozen copies, but you can have different colours on the same sheet of paper. The copies are often fuzzy and blotched.

Ink duplicators produce better quality copies but are more expensive than spirit duplicators. They will produce hundreds of copies of the original. Again, you have to type the original onto a special piece of paper — a *stencil*. However, an *electronic stencil cutter* will copy any document, even some photographs, onto a stencil.

Once you have produced the required number of copies of each page of your publication, you have to put the pages together in the right order and bind them in some way. There are machines which will help to do this.

Collators

Collating is putting the pages together in the right order. Instead of having to take one page from each pile of copies in the correct order, the machine does this for you. Each pile of copies is put in a separate tray, and the machine produces the complete publication ready for binding.

Joggers

A jogger straightens the pages by jogging them together before they are put into the binder.

Binding machines

These bind the pages together. There are many different types. Some use special glues or chemicals. Others attach a metal or plastic binding strip which pierces through the edges of the pages.

A long-armed stapler will staple a publication together without creasing the pages.

Finding out more about reprographics

you can find out more by visiting:

- the reprographics facility of your school, college or local authority,
- a high street print shop,
- office equipment shops and exhibitions,
- office technology exhibitions,

and by looking at office equipment catalogues and leaflets.

Desktop publishing

The best office reprographics are always much poorer than real printing, such as you find in books and magazines. However, it is now possible to achieve *real* printing quality on office microcomputers. This is called desktop publishing.

Desktop publishing software allows you to design a page on the computer screen. You can combine different layouts (columns and blocks of writing) and many different sizes and styles of lettering (different *fonts*). You can include diagrams, graphs, charts, and pictures to produce a very professional-looking document.

This can be printed out on an ordinary computer printer which has a ribbon like a typewriter. But to achieve printing quality, the computer needs a special *laser* or *ink-jet* printer. A laser printer uses a laser light beam on light-sensitive paper. An ink jet printer squirts the ink onto the paper.

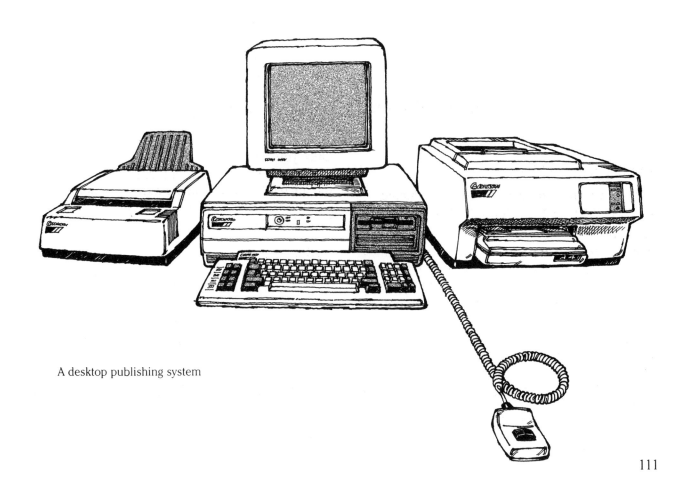

A desktop publishing system

REFERENCE SECTION

Outline of the economy

This outline summarises and explains the conclusions which can be drawn from the Standard of Living game.

Goods and services

The economy produces the goods and services we enjoy.

Goods
TV set
clothes
furniture
food
..... and house, car, and all other personal possessions.

Services
haircut
TV programme
..... and education, medical care, police forces, public transport, shops, parks, cinemas, street-lighting, drains, etc.

How goods and services are produced

Obviously, all these goods and services do not simply happen to exist ...

1 Labour

... they have all been produced from the world about us by people's work, by labour. Everything, all wealth and possessions, has been produced by someone's work.

2 Specialisation and trade

If each person tries to produce everything for themselves, they produce very little. People produce more if they *specialise* in producing just certain things and *trade* with other people who specialise in producing other things.

The modern economy

In modern Britain, we have a very high standard of living because we have acquired vast amounts of capital: machines, computers, factories, roads, railways, power-stations, etc.

3 Money

Trading requires *money*. Money stands for real things, for real goods and services. For more information on money see page 70.

4 Capital

People can produce *much* more if they have tools, especially if the tools can be power-driven.

Machines, factories, computers and transportation systems are simply very big and powerful tools. The name for all these is *capital*.

Primary Sector Produces the raw materials. (metals, wood, food, fuel, etc.)	*Manufacturing Sector* Turns the raw materials into goods.	*Service Sector* Produces services. (shops which supply goods to the consumer, garages and repair services, education, medical care, public transport, banking, insurance, post and telephone, etc.)
A highly developed economy, such as Britain's, usually has a large service sector.		

The role of business, administration and offices is to organise all this economic activity.

How the goods and services are shared out depends on how much the government controls the economy.

The market economy

economy uncontrolled by government

5 What is produced and what prices are paid is decided simply by market forces — how people behave in a market. If people want more of something the price goes up so the producers supply more. If the *demand* for eggs drops, then so will the price, and therefore the *supply* of eggs; the producer will supply something else that is wanted, eg feathers. The Standard of Living Game was a market economy; it shows what happens in such an economy.

6
- **In theory** the market is an efficient way of organising the economy. The chance to earn money motivates people to work hard. People are free to work as they want and to buy what they want.
- **But there are winners and losers** — a few rich people and many poor people — a very unequal society. Clever or lucky people become rich, and less able or less lucky people become poor. The inequality tends to reinforce itself. The children of the rich start with advantages and privileges which others do not have, eg private schools.
- **Freedom only for the rich** Poor people have no freedom of choice to buy what they want (eg private schooling, private medicine). High unemployment means no freedom to work.
- **Not efficient** The few most successful businesses become so big and powerful that they may control the market (*monopolies*), so the customers have less choice about prices or what is produced. It also seems to be unstable, because it produces periods of high unemployment.

The planned economy

economy is planned and organised by the government

The government decides what should be produced, what prices should be charged, and how much pay people should receive.

- **In theory** a planned economy makes the best use of resources (eg deciding to build factories and schools rather than unnecessary luxury goods). It should be a fairer society because the Government can share out income and wealth equally, and can make sure everyone has a job.
- **But it is not efficient:** without the incentive of making money people work less hard. A very large and slow administration system develops.
- **Unpopular:** people do not like governments telling them what to do (what to produce and what they can buy).
- **Unequal:** the people in power tend to give themselves more money and privileges than other people receive.

Britain's economy

In practice, most economies are not simply market economies or planned economies, but have some aspects of both. Communist countries, like Russia and China, basically have planned economies. Western countries, like Britain, basically have market economies but with a certain amount of government planning and control, so they are sometimes called mixed economies.

In a mixed economy, the part that the Government controls on behalf of the public is called the *public sector*, and the part that is left to private individuals to do as they like is called the *private sector*. The effect of this economy is shown on the next three spreads.

Who owns the wealth

How wealth is shared out in Britain.

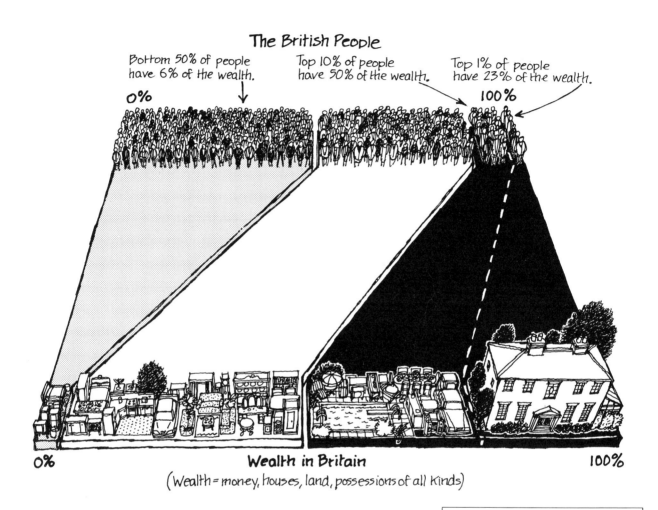

7 Winners and losers in the British economy

Imagine a one-hour parade in which each person's income is shown by their height. A person with a small wage is shown as a small person; a highly paid person is shown as a giant. The whole population of Britain walks past in one hour. This is what it would look like.

From P. Donaldson Economics of the Real World *Penguin 1984.*

NOTE THAT it is not until 45 minutes have passed, that people of normal height appear in the parade. In other words, three-quarters of the British population receive less than an equal share of incomes.

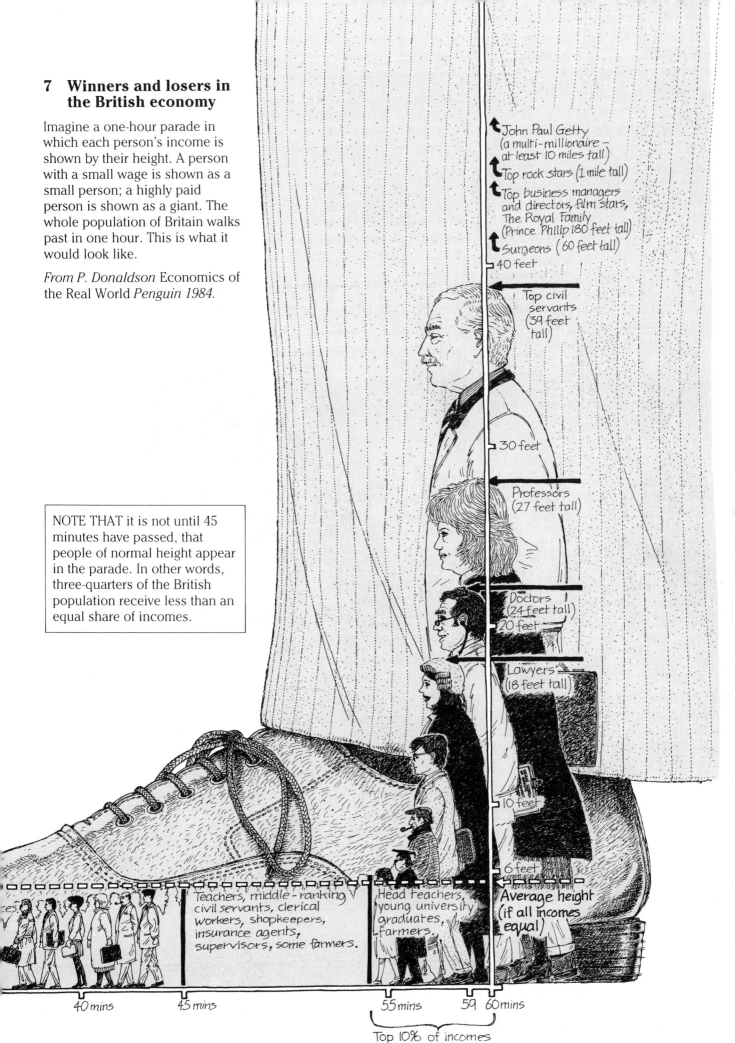

Central and local government

Central government

Central government provides services for the whole country.

The Government

The Government spends tax money to provide services, (eg the army, roads, the National Health Service). The political party with the most MPs (Members of Parliament) in the Commons forms the Government (also called the Cabinet). The leader of the party becomes the Prime Minister and appoints about twenty other MPs of that party to be the ministers in charge of the different departments of the Government. The Government meets in the Cabinet Room in the Prime Minister's offices at 10 Downing Street to decide what laws should be made and how tax money should be spent.

The main Government departments and Cabinet Ministers are:
The **Foreign Office**, headed by the Foreign Secretary, which deals with embassies, and Britain's relations with other countries.
The **Treasury**, headed by the Chancellor of the Exchequer, which controls taxes, money, and the economy.
The **Home Office**, headed by the Home Secretary, which deals with the police, prisons, law and order.
Education and Science
Health and Social Security
The **Environment**, which covers roads, building, etc.
Employment, which deals with Job Centres and YTS.

Parliament

Parliament makes laws and fixes taxes, such as income tax, VAT and other taxes. There are two parts, the *House of Commons* and the *House of Lords.*

The Commons has 650 MPs who represent constituencies all over Britain. MPs usually belong to a political party (Conservative, Labour, etc). The Commons has to be re-elected every five years. The Lords is not elected, but it has no real power.
The Government proposes new laws, including taxes. A proposed law, called a *Bill*, is debated in great detail by both Houses. When it passes the final vote, it becomes part of the law and is called an *Act*.

The Civil Service

This consists of Government employees. Government Ministers make the major decisions. The detailed running of the Government departments is carried out by thousands of Government employees called *Civil Servants*. Most Government departments have their headquarters in Whitehall.

Local Government
provides local services

Each part of Britain has its own local government, called a *Local Authority*, or *local council*, to organise local services: police, schools and colleges, the fire brigade, council houses, street-lighting and cleaning, libraries, social services, etc. The structure of local government is very similar to that of the central government, but the names are different.

Elected members, *Councillors*, have council meetings to make local laws and decide how to use tax money for local services. The Local Authority is divided into different departments: Education, Social Services, etc., run by employees called *local government officers*.

Types of Local Authorities

In England and Wales, large city areas are called Metropolitan Counties and are divided into Metropolitan District Councils (called Borough Councils in London).

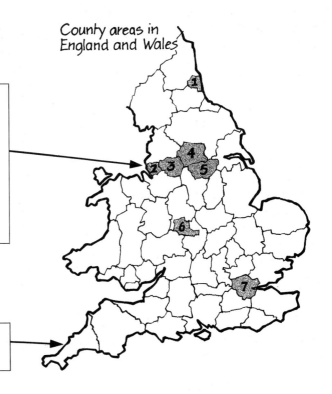

Shaded areas are Metropolitan Counties:
1. Tyne & Wear
2. Merseyside
3. Greater Manchester
4. West Yorkshire
5. South Yorkshire
6. West Midlands
7. London

Elsewhere there are County Councils which are divided into smaller District Councils.

Eg Cornwall, which is divided into 6 District Councils.

Scotland and Northern Ireland have similar structures. Scotland also has its own system of law.

Local Authorities get half their money from central government — the Rate Support Grant. They get the other half of their money by charging local taxes, either on buildings, the Rates, or on people, the Poll Tax. In a Rates tax, the owners of big houses and buildings have to pay more tax than the owners of small houses and buildings. In the Poll tax, every person pays the same amount whether they are rich or poor. So the Rates makes people more equal, whereas the Poll tax favours the rich people and makes life hard for the poor people.

Political beliefs

Political beliefs are often discussed in terms of *Left* and *Right*. These are two basically different views of society. The Left believes that a society of rich and poor, winners and losers, is unfair and wrong. The Right believes that it is unfair to interfere: people should be allowed to win and lose.

LEFT (Equality)	RIGHT (Competition)
People should be equal. They should have equal opportunities in life, equal power, equal standards of living. A society of rich and poor is unfair.	People should be allowed to win and lose. It is fair that clever, strong, or lucky people should be rich and others poorer. It is unfair to stop people winning.
Freedom — being free to do things, and not being prevented by lack of money or power. (Poor people are not free to go to private schools or private hospitals.)	Freedom — being left alone, no interference, as few laws as possible. (People should be free to avoid hospital waiting lists by paying to be a private patient.)
SO	SO

LEFT:

- Laws to give people freedom from unfair treatment.
  Equal opportunities and sex discrimination laws. Laws to protect employees; legal minimum wages, maternity leave, health and safety requirements. Laws which help trade unions to operate. (see p. 122)
- Planned Economy (see page 113)
  Business organisations should be owned and controlled by everyone involved in them.
  Public sector organisations (see p. 119). But a completely planned economy run entirely by the government can be inefficient and unpopular, so there is a need for greater democracy (co-operatives, and local community planning and control).
  Taxes needed for public sector businesses (education, National Health Service, etc). Rich should pay more tax than poor, for example, rates tax (see p. 117).
- Goods and services, money and wealth should be shared out equally.
  For example, medical care, education and legal services provided to everyone as a right.
- Greater democracy: more power-sharing, voting and representation.
  More local community planning and decision-making, for example, all workers in a business should be involved in decision-making, as in trade unions.

RIGHT:

- As few laws as possible.
  Every extra law is another restriction on someone's freedom. Employers should be able to employ whom they want, when and how they want. Employers should be able to pay employees whatever they will accept. Laws which restrict trade unions, which ban strikes and picketing. (see p. 121)
- Market Economy (see page 113)
  People who have the wealth or ability to set up businesses should own them, control them, and keep the profits.
  Private sector organisations (see p. 119). Privatising nationalised industries because the private sector can be more efficient (but then profits no longer go to the community as a whole but only to the shareholders).
  Keep taxes as low as possible, so people can choose what to spend their money on. Rich and poor should pay the same amount of taxes, for example, poll tax (see p. 117).
- People should only get the goods and services they can pay for.
  For example, private medicine, education, legal services, etc.
- Respect for authority: managers should be allowed to manage.
  Managers have the right and the expertise to make the decisions. Others should accept them and co-operate, otherwise the business becomes inefficient.

```
         Communist        Labour      SLD       Conservative      Fascist
                                      SDP                         National Front
                                                                  Nazi
LEFT  ←——————————————————————————————————————————————————————————————————→  RIGHT
         (planned economy)  ←——————————————————————→  (market economy)
              SOCIALISM                                   CAPITALISM
```

NOTE This is only a rough guide. Political beliefs are very complicated and this chart only shows some typical patterns. There are many exceptions and contradictions, and political beliefs often become confused in practice. For example, trade unions are illegal in Poland, which is a left-wing, communist country. Many people would say there is no real democracy in communist countries. Again, in the USA, a right-wing capitalist country, there are many laws guaranteeing equal opportunities.

Organisations in the British economy

There are two parts to the British economy: the private sector and the public sector.

Private Sector

Private individuals owning and operating businesses.

These are organisations set up to make money for the owners of the business. The profits go to the owners, not the people who work in the business.

People

A person can own and run a business by themselves, called a *sole trader* business, or with one or more partners, called a *partnership*, eg small shops, builders, plumbers, garages, doctors and accountants. These are usually very small businesses, although they may include some employees as well as the sole trader or partners.

Trading as a person can be difficult and risky, because your business is you. You are personally *liable*, that is, responsible, for any business debts. So if business goes badly, you may have to sell your house and car and all your possessions to pay off the business debts. For the same reason, it is difficult to borrow much money to expand the business.

Companies

If you make your business into a company, it is separate from you. Any business debts are not your personal debts, and you do not have to sell all your possessions to pay off your business debts. Your *liability*, ie your responsibility for business debts, is *limited* to the amount of money you have put into the business. This is why companies are called *limited companies*, because the owners have only *limited liability* for the business debts.

The amount of money you put into the business is called your *share* of the business. So the *shareholders* are the owners of the business. If the business fails, you will not get your share back because it will go towards paying off the business debts. But if the business goes well, you receive some of the profits each year, a *dividend*. The company can raise money to expand by inviting people to buy more shares.

Private Limited Companies (Ltd) can only offer shares *privately* to family and friends. Such companies must have Ltd in their name. Many small and medium-sized businesses are private limited companies.

Public Limited Companies (plc) can offer shares to the *public* through the Stock Exchange, and must have plc in their name. These are giant companies, usually well-known names employing thousands of people, eg Kodak, Shell, ICI, Ford. The biggest public limited companies are called multinationals because they operate in many countries around the world. They sometimes have more money and resources than whole countries. They are immensely powerful, and can influence the lives of thousands or millions of people who have no say in the decisions of these multinationals.

Non-profit-making organisations

Some private sector organisations are not intended to make a profit for the owners, but to benefit everyone involved in them:
co-operatives (all the employees are also owners),
building societies,
trade unions and professional associations,
charities and pressure groups.

Public Sector

Organisations owned by the public and run by the Government.

These are organisations not set up to make money, but to provide a public service for everyone. Instead of belonging to some private individuals, they belong to the whole public, and any profits they make go to the whole public.

Government departments

For example, the Department of Health and Social Security, which provides the National Health Service, the Department of the Environment, which provides roads, buildings, etc. The money for these services comes from taxes such as income tax and VAT.

Local authorities

These provide local services, such as schools, council houses, libraries, fire services, street-lighting, etc. The money for these services comes partly from the local authority taxes on buildings, the *rates*, and partly from central government from income tax, VAT, etc.

Nationalised industries

These are public corporations and regional authorities, for example, British Rail, the BBC, the Post Office, British Coal. These are not paid for out of taxes. These goods and services are sold to the customers. Any profits go back into the industry to improve services or lower prices.

Structure of organisations

The structure of an organisation is the way it is organised internally: what departments or sections it has, and how the different departments relate to each other.

All organisations are set up to achieve a purpose, eg making something, selling something or providing a service. How they are structured depends on what they do, who owns them, and how many people are involved.

Typical structure of a large Public Limited Company (PLC)

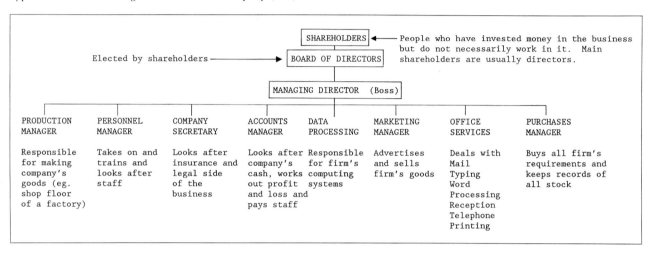

Smaller businesses have to look after all the above aspects of their business but do not have separate departments employing specialist qualified personnel.

Typical structure of a local authority

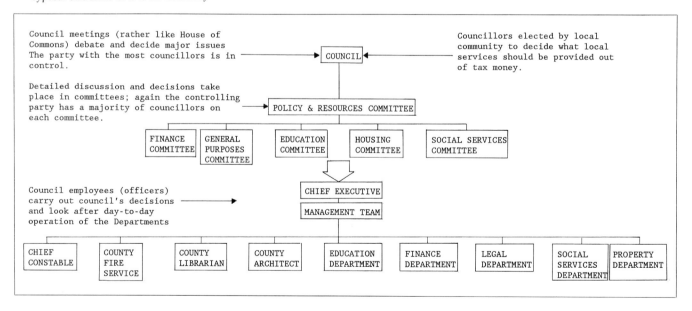

Trade unions

Trade unions are employees acting together *in a united way* to bargain with the employer. This acting together, or *solidarity*, is very important for unions because the union's only bargaining strength is that *all* the employees could refuse to co-operate and stop working. Otherwise the employees are almost powerless. Unions bargain for better pay and working conditions, and give the employees some influence in the running of their workplace. Unions are democratic, unlike company management. For further details see page 95.

Recent laws have restricted trade union power because the government believed that some unions had grown too powerful in bargaining for better wages. (See pages 114–5) for information on wages, ie income in Britain.)

Employment Act 1980:

- limits number of people allowed to picket,
- forbids one union to strike in solidarity with another union,
- allows employees to opt out of closed shop arrangements,
- provides government money for ballots.

Employment Act 1982   *States:*

- when a closed shop agreement is made, it must be as a result of a ballot of employees,
- unions are liable for damages up to £250,000 if they defy the courts.

Trade Union Act 1984   *States:*

- a secret ballot of all members must be taken before strike action,
- all union officials in National Executive must be re-elected by secret ballot every five years,
- members must be balloted to see if they still wish to contribute funds to political parties.

Some technical terms

ACAS   Arbitration, Conciliatory and Advisory Service — an organisation which helps to settle industrial disputes.
arbitration   having an independent person or people acting as judge during a dispute (eg over a pay rise).
ballot   a proper vote (each person writes down their vote in private on a ballot paper, instead of a public show of hands where people might feel intimidated).
blacklegs or scabs   employees who keep working instead of joining in a strike.
blue-collar workers   people who do manual jobs such as working with machinery.
closed shop   a workplace where all the employees must be union members.
industrial action   a general name for a strike or a work to rule.
picketing   persuading fellow-workers not to work when there is a strike.

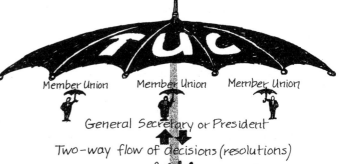

political levy   money contributed by unions to a political party, usually the Labour Party. (Companies usually contribute money to the Conservative Party.)
solidarity   acting together. This is the basis of all union action.
strike   refusing to work.
unofficial strike   employees going on strike without the agreement of their union.
victimisation   unfair treatment (eg if a worker is sacked for taking part in union activities).
white-collar workers   people who have an office-type job.
work to rule/go slow   refusing to do more than minimum duties.

Employment law

The law gives you various rights at work, particularly relating to unfair treatment, and health and safety.

Contract of employment

When you accept a job offer, you and your employer have made a contract. The contract is important because it specifies what your rights and duties are at work, and what can happen if you are in dispute with your employer. Not all of the contract is in writing. The contract includes what was said and agreed at the job interview, as well as a written statement. The employer must, by law, give you a written statement within 13 weeks of your starting work. It must provide details of:

- The employer's name.
- The date on which you started work.
- Your pay: how much, how it is calculated, and whether payment is weekly or monthly, etc.
- Hours of work, including details of overtime and overtime pay.
- Holidays and holiday pay.
- Sickness and sick pay.
- Pension schemes, if there are any.
- Length of notice.
- Grievance and disciplinary procedures (for dealing with disputes between you and your employer).
- Your job title.

There may also be other written statements, such as a letter of appointment offering you the job, or a job description.

Unfair dismissal

Full-time workers have some legal protection against unfair dismissal if they have worked for the firm for at least a year, or two years in the case of a firm with less than 21 employees. Protection against dismissal for trade union membership applies as soon as the person begins work.

Discrimination and equal opportunities

Race and sex It is illegal for an employer to discriminate against you because of your race or sex or because you are married or unmarried. This applies to job interviews and appointments, pay and promotion. (*Race Relations Act 1976, Sex Discrimination Act 1975, Equal Pay Act 1970.*)

Gays, lesbians and disabled people are often discriminated against by employers, but there is no law which specifically forbids such discrimination. However, trade unions can help in some cases.

For further information contact:

| The Equal Opportunities Commission
Overseas House
Quay Street
Manchester M3 3HN | The Commission for Racial Equality
Elliot House
10–12 Allington Street
London SW1 4LA | National Council for Civil Liberties
21 Tabard Street
London SE1 4LA |

Health and safety at work

Every year, thousands of people are killed or seriously injured at work. It is very important to be aware of health and safety at work. There are several laws which lay down minimum safety standards for the protection of employers and employees.

1 *The Factories Act 1961* applies to factory employees.
The Office, Shops & Railway Premises Act 1963 applies to these workplaces and covers overcrowding, temperature, ventilation, lighting, toilets, washing facilities and seating.

2 *The Health and Safety at Work Act 1974* applies to *all* workplaces: factories, offices, hospitals, transport, shops and all other premises, including schools and colleges.

   Employers have to:
   - Provide a safe working environment: safe procedures, safe equipment and competent staff.
   - Provide a written policy statement on the health and safety of the employees, and also display the relevant sections of the 1961 and 1963 Acts in the case of those workplaces.
   - Allow for the appointment of a trade union health and safety representative. It is very important to have a trade union representative. They have the right to get information from the management, to inspect the workplaces at least once every three months, and to call in the health and safety inspector if necessary.

   Employees have to act safely. They must follow the correct procedures, use safety guards, etc.

   The Health and Safety Executive employ inspectors who make sure the law is carried out, but the most effective part of this law is the trade union involvement.

   If you have an accident at work report it to the person who keeps the accident book or to the personnel officer. Even small injuries should be reported in case they turn out to be serious. If you notice any safety hazards, report them to the trade union safety representative.

Trade union membership

Although the law provides you some basic protection against unfair treatment by an employer, trade union membership gives you better protection (see *Your Rights at Work* details below). A trade union will not only help you to get the protection which the law provides but it can also negotiate directly with the employer to provide much better protection. To join a trade union, see the trade union representative at work. If there is no trade union at your workplace, contact the Trades Union Congress (the TUC), Great Russell Street, London WC1 who will advise you. It is illegal for an employer to victimise an employee for trying to join a trade union.

For more detailed information on all these topics, see the National Council for Civil Liberties handbook, *Your Rights at Work* (B Birtles and P Hewitt, NCCL, 1983) which is available at most bookshops and libraries.

Consumer law

By exchanging money for goods when you buy something, you are making a *contract* with the trader.

Under this *contract of sale* the trader has certain responsibilities which are laid down in the 1979 Sale of Goods Act.

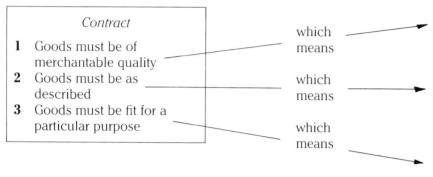

Contract

1. Goods must be of merchantable quality — which means → The item must not be broken or damaged and must work properly.
2. Goods must be as described — which means → Goods must be as they are described by the trader or on the packet. If the box says 'pink clock', a blue clock would not be acceptable. A viscose scarf cannot be marked 'silk'.
3. Goods must be fit for a particular purpose — which means → If you ask for a saw to cut metal, one to cut wood would not be 'fit for its purpose'.

If you buy goods and find they are not satisfactory for any of the above reasons, then the retailer has *broken* the *contract* they made with you. You should return the goods to the shop where you bought them as soon as possible.

Returning goods to the retailer

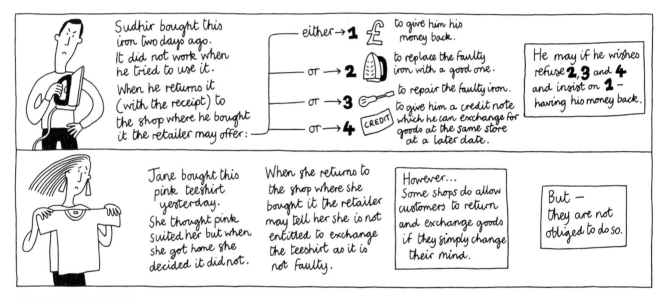

Sudhir bought this iron two days ago. It did not work when he tried to use it. When he returns it (with the receipt) to the shop where he bought it the retailer may offer:
- either → **1** to give him his money back.
- or → **2** to replace the faulty iron with a good one.
- or → **3** to repair the faulty iron.
- or → **4** to give him a credit note which he can exchange for goods at the same store at a later date.

He may if he wishes refuse **2, 3** and **4** and insist on **1** — having his money back.

Jane bought this pink teeshirt yesterday. She thought pink suited her but when she got home she decided it did not. When she returns to the shop where she bought it the retailer may tell her she is not entitled to exchange the teeshirt as it is not faulty.

However... Some shops do allow customers to return and exchange goods if they simply change their mind.

But — they are not obliged to do so.

Getting more information

You can get more information, about your rights and about consumer advice and protection organisations, from:

Libraries
Citizens' Advice Bureaux
Consumer Advice Centres
} See the Community Pages of your *Thomson Local Directory*

Information Leaflets. These are usually available in libraries and Citizens' Advice Bureax. If not, write to the following bodies:

The Office of Fair Trading
Room 310
15–25 Bream's Buildings
London EC4 A1PR
(or your local office)

The Department of Trade
Room 207
Gaywood House
29 Great Peter Street
London SW1P 3LW

Her Majesty's Stationery Office
49 High Holborn
London WC1V 6HB
(or your local office)

Notes for the teacher

How to organise the Leisure Centre simulation

The Leisure Centre activity is a simulation exercise. It provides the students with the opportunity to use their newly-established organisation to operate an imaginary leisure centre.

It is an extremely flexible simulation, offering a great variety of activities and possibilities. The Leisure Centre with its administrative procedures is rather like a film set, or the setting for a TV soap opera. It simply requires the plot, a sequence of events, characters and developments, to be fed into it. The plot can be a humdrum series of routine bookings and membership applications. Indeed, it may be best to begin this way so that the students can familiarise themselves with the procedures. But it will become much more interesting if, as in soap operas, some of the members begin to take on recognisable personalities and a story begins to develop. So, for example, a persistent late-payer, who writes letters of complaint whenever the Hall is booked for five-a-side football rather than badminton, could marry one of the bar staff, and hold the wedding reception in the Hall, prompting complaints from the football enthusiasts.

The way in which the Leisure Centre and its procedures are used is determined by the information fed into the Leisure Centre organisation. You may well want to design some or all of this information yourself. An example of how the Leisure Centre can be used, and how the basic simulation of routine bookings and memberships can be set up and operated, is given below, together with some suggestions for subsequent developments.

Purpose of simulation

The simulation provides practice and experience in the following areas:

Organisational structure. This helps students to understand the roles of different departments and how the departments support and depend on each other.
Administrative procedures both within and between departments. *Routine operation* of
> mail procedures
> telephone messages and personal callers at Reception
> detailed record-keeping, using charts and files, filing
> invoicing (and ensuring payments are kept up-to-date)
> business correspondence (standard letters, covering letters, circular letters and responses to specific queries).

Outline of the simulation

The simulation is simply concerned with memberships and bookings of the Leisure Centre, and the record-keeping, calculations and correspondence that this generates. It operates as follows.

Reception
Receives booking and membership requests which it transcribes onto the appropriate forms and sends to Records.
Receives other enquiries which it directs to the appropriate department.
These requests and enquiries may be in the form of letters, recorded telephone messages or personal callers.
Types letters for Administration.

Records
Accepts or rejects membership and booking requests, according to availability. Accepted ones are passed to Accounts for invoicing; rejected ones are sent to Administration which informs the applicant by letter.
Deals with queries about bookings and memberships.

Accounts
Produces invoices based on the accepted membership and booking requests. These are then passed to Administration which provides a covering letter.

Administration
Produces letters to deal with the rejected booking and membership requests received from Records, and the invoices received from Accounts.
Responds to any other letters received by the Leisure Centre, for example, letters querying invoices, or letters of complaint.

Operating the simulation

In the simulation, each day lasts an hour, and it is assumed that the date at the start of the simulation is 1 November. So if the simulation starts at 9.00 am, 1 November lasts from 9.00–10.00, 2 November from 10.00–11,00, 3 November from 11.00–12.00, and so on.

Although the Centre's membership is assumed to be almost full, the simulation only requires the details of 48 members.

To start the simulation:

Reception and Typing needs a bundle of inputs, that is, booking requests and membership requests in the form of letters, completed forms, recorded telephone messages, perhaps role-played personal visits.

Three sets of membership details, ie current membership forms, are needed. These are for Administration, Records and for two or three students in a separate room acting as the Centre's members.

To keep the simulation operating, it is necessary to have a continual stream of inputs, not just booking and membership requests, but also complaints about invoice mistakes, double-bookings and other matters, and enquiries about special events, etc., and the outputs (letters and invoices), need to be responded to. This can be arranged by having two or three students in a separate room playing the part of the Centre's membership. They check each invoice, sending payment if it is correct (Monopoly money or a cheque), and a letter of complaint if it is not; they respond to other letters and they make new requests for bookings and membership, for which purpose they need membership details. These students can also deliver some of their inputs in the form of role-played personal visits to Reception.

Two or three students in a separate room act as the Centre's members (making booking and membership requests and responding to invoices and letters).

How to prepare the inputs

The easiest way to prepare the necessary information to be fed into the organisation is to ask the students to produce it before the simulation begins. The following instructions produce a set of initial inputs which will include the necessary double-bookings, over-subscribed membership categories and out-of-date memberships.

Membership details Ask the class to fill out 48 Membership forms including the 'Office Use Only' sections, using the following membership numbers. Divide the class into four groups and give each group 12 forms and its allocation of numbers to use. Since three sets of the membership details are needed, ask the students to complete the 48 forms in triplicate. This means that, in total, the class needs $48 \times 3 = 144$ blank forms.

	Membership numbers
OFF-PEAK Membership	124–135
PEAK Membership	282–293
FAMILY Membership	388–399
CONCESSION Membership	465–476

The dates on which the memberships begin should be drawn evenly from the following periods:

a) 29–31 October

b) 1–3 November

c) 4–18 November

d) Any other date

(Tell the students they must use a date from a different period for each form, as far as possible.) All other details on the membership forms can be invented, but must be consistent with the existing details.

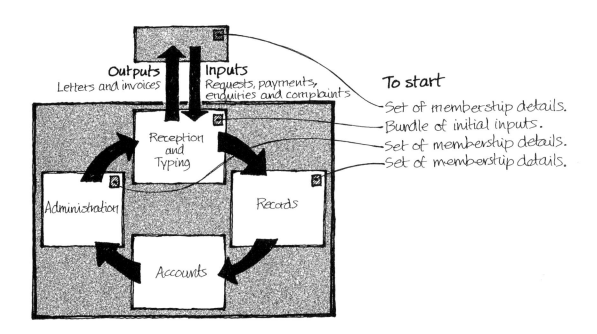

Initial inputs Ask each student to take TWO of the membership forms they have just filled it, and make SIX booking requests in total on behalf of those two members (eg four requests for one member, and two requests for the other one).

Two of the requests should be on Booking Request forms, two in the form of letters addressed to Reception, and two in the form of a simple note. These notes can then be converted into recorded telephone messages on a cassette-recorder, or used for role-played personal visits to Reception.

The booking requests should all be for dates in the period 1–14 November.

Finally, ask each student to make an application for membership, particularly PEAK or FAMILY membership. These applications can be in the form of a letter, a note, a telephone message, or a Membership form.

Suggestions for subsequent development

The simulation will become more enjoyable, and more life-like, if recognisable characters and a story-line begin to appear. These developments can either be left to the ingenuity of the two or three students playing the part of the Leisure Centre's members, perhaps working within an outline plot provided by the teachers, or the teachers can prepare the necessary letters and requests and add them to the inputs at the appropriate times. The role-playing students can role-play the characters.

1 **Characters** Habitual late-payers, persistent moaners (about opening times, not being given reduced prices although not entitled to them), someone who keeps making mistakes in payments or bookings, a Film Society Secretary who will only book the Club Room for film shows if there is no Table Tennis tournaments next door because of the noise and crowds, estranged lovers who do not want to be booked into the Fitness Room at the same time, etc.

2 **Story-line events** Friction between clubs and societies, eg, a Chess Club Secretary who negotiates a block booking for Club Room 1 and then does not use the room although other clubs and societies would like to use it, a member is accused of abusive behaviour while using the Fitness Room but claims he was not using the room on that day — Records department asked to confirm etc.

Special functions: table tennis tournament with visiting teams and sandwiches in Club Room 1 afterwards, wedding receptions, discotheques, live bands, etc.